RELUCTANT Q

BY

GEORGE HENRY SPILL

AND NICK SPILL

Reluctant Q / George Spill and Nick Spill – 1st U.S. Edition

Reluctant Q

Library of Congress Cataloging-in-Publication Data
Spill, George. Spill, Nick
World War II, 1939-1945 – Campaigns – Burma
World War II, 1939-1945 – Personal narratives, British
Great Britain, Army – Royal Artillery – Biography
Soldiers, Great Britain – Biography

ISBN: 978-0-9839080-6-7 e-book
978-0-9839080-7-4 print version

Book Cover and Design: Damonza
Cover Photo: © Crown Copyright. IWM. The Battle of Imphal-Kohima, March-July 1944. The remains of Japanese dead, equipment and caved in bunkers in the Shenam area.

DISCLAIMER: Some names and identifying details have been changed or omitted to protect the privacy of individuals and their surviving families.

More information about Reluctant Q can be seen at
http://nickspill.com
and
http://nickspill.blogspot.com

The events and characters are factual but identities have been changed with due respect to any living relations and survivors of my old unit.

George Henry Spill
"Q" Quartermaster
Rank on Class C release from the British Army
Battery Quartermaster Sergeant (B.Q.M.S.)
123rd Battery Officer Cadet Training Unit Royal Artillery
(123 OCTU RA)

Army Number: 1091472
Dates of service: October 17th 1940 to September 26th 1945

DEDICATION

To my wife for her forbearance and support and to my son Nick who gave me the idea to write this book and to all the men who I served with who never came back.

ONE

WE ARE ON a hill position half way between Tamu in Burma and Palel on the border of the plains of Imphal, which commands the main highway into India. The place is known locally as Tengnoupal but that doesn't mean anything, as there's nothing here to identify it, only jungle. We are about halfway up the hill from the jeep track, which is the main road, and have a commanding view east and south to a great range of hills, which seem endless. The nearest is about half a mile away and we believe, occupied by Japanese infantry. Between the nearest hills and our gun position is a valley, which drops at least a thousand feet into dense jungle and is almost impassable.

The time is early June 1944, and as yet there is no news of a second front in Europe. During the past nine months we have been digging holes all over Northern Burma in constant retreat. From the great Chindwin River, up over the disease-infected Kabaw Valley, we have withdrawn to our present position, our ranks and equipment thinning every day by constant action and disease. The Japanese have roadblocks everywhere, cutting us off from the outside world. But our infantry hold the hills to the south commanding the only track, preventing the enemy infiltrating further. Our orders are that there will be no further retreat. We are to defend to the last man. We hope that when the coming monsoon breaks it will also stop the enemy. The Japs have brought guns forward and large shells, believed to be 150 mm caliber, have been exploding in the valley below us, but they obviously cannot get the range and all they are doing is scything away large areas of jungle for no apparent purpose. The monsoon therefore, is the better of the two evils and once the storms and heavy rains commence everything will come to a halt. By the way, our unit is the remains of a battery of Medium Artillery, the only Medium 5.5-inch guns in northern Burma and I am battery quartermaster sergeant.

All the men refer to me as Q.

Our only news of what is happening on the other side of the world is what we hear on Radio India, when reception is favorable. But they never mention this front, confirming we are indeed the Forgotten Army. Bitter experience has taught us to dig and get below ground as quickly as possible at every move and we are thankful that the ground here is soft and yielding to the spade. We dig non-stop until we are comfortably underground. Our system of six-foot deep trenches and covered Bren gun pits are as good as any.

We have cleared the bush, laid coiled barbed wire around our perimeter, put in Panji stakes and booby traps with trip wires and are confident we will be able to withstand an attack. The gunners remain with their guns at all times and have telephone connections with our command post as do the two Bren gun posts commanding the perimeters protecting each gun whilst, in turn, the field telephone is connected through to Brigade H.Q.

To maintain silence, night and day, we have a system of communication, man to man, consisting of lengths of old telephone wire stretching from a Bren gun post to men in support, who attach the wire to their wrists or ankles to be pulled by whoever gives the alarm. During the hours of darkness those on duty are able to alert all the men in their section in complete silence.

For many months now we automatically stand-to for an hour before dawn and an hour after sunset which means we are ready in our trenches for an attack. It gets dark quickly in the Tropics.

I pick up the end of the wire in the slit trench and attach it to my wrist after giving the wire one pull to signal I have taken my place, the gunner on duty acknowledges in the same manner. I have another wire that extends to my dugout. I attach the wire to my ankle hoping to get a decent sleep, but it doesn't always work, as I was once pulled half way out of my trench before I woke up.

I have an empty ammunition box in the slit trench and I sit down, light a cigarette and await the signal to stand-down. It is hot and humid. Even though it's still daylight the mosquitoes have begun to attack. There is no breeze and I keep my head below ground. There are Jap sharpshooters out there but I don't care about the smoke. I inhale deeply and wave my arms about to disperse the smoke, as smoking is prohibited during stand-to and cigarettes are in very short supply. It's been reasonably quiet today and as it gets dark the atmosphere is eerie, in contrast to times when the world is blasted apart and men die around me. I wonder whether it will be my turn soon.

I think we are going to be kept awake all night again, waiting for the action. It is too still and I inhale my cigarette. I have a crate of grenades next to me, a Sten gun with a pile of loaded magazines. I have seen what they have done to prisoners and know it's either them or me.

When we first arrived in Burma, a Japanese Zero buzzed our unit. Instead of the fighter plane firing at us, it dropped a load of color photographs. When we picked them up we saw British prisoners of war tied up and kneeling on the ground beheaded by Japanese officers with long swords. Each photo was more horrendous than the last and depicted a variety of decapitations. They were designed to demoralize us. Instead we became mad with rage and realized we could never surrender. We had to fight to the death.

The enemy has been known to use all manner of tricks to discover our positions often keeping up a constant barrage of dialogue in English over loudspeakers. A strange voice, obviously Japanese, but with a fake English accent, would either taunt us or promise all sorts of goodies if we surrender. "Hey Tommy! Your wife is with Yankees. She getting fucked by

Yankees!" Tonight, there was no voice coming from the jungle. The photographs of the captured haunt us.

Sound travels great distances up here in the hills and there is no telling how far away the enemy is. Just one rifle shot on a night such as this will echo back and forth many times in the valleys and hundreds of men will stand and wait. As it is, the quietness has engulfed me and I am alone in the world, my thoughts drifting and dreaming. I light another cigarette from the glowing butt and wonder how long our supplies will last. We consumed our emergency rations three weeks ago and have had nothing since. There hasn't been an airdrop for weeks and even if the R.A.F. dropped more supplies, they would fall in the jungle out of our reach.

Clearing the roadblocks on the Tamu to Palel Road, caused by rain and landslides seems an impossible task, as the Japs are too numerous. So we are going to be even hungrier. We know they are in the jungle just past our clearing, watching us, observing the smoke from our cigarettes, calculating where our gun emplacements are, the arc of our firing positions, how many guns we have.

My thoughts start to drift. I remember friends, now dead and I wish I could turn the clock back. It's the uncertainty that gets me down. We have been in action for two years and as we are the only Medium Artillery in this war zone there is to be no relief. If I were serving a prison sentence I would know roughly when I would be released. The chances of getting out of here alive seem remote and a passage on a boat home, an impossible fantasy.

It's been four months since the last delivery of mail from home and a similar time since we have sent any. Add to that the three months it takes the mail to reach us from England and no wonder some have given up hope and are depressed. For a number of reasons I feel empty inside. It's difficult to explain my feelings. If I give vent to how I feel I could endanger the lives of others, so there seems nothing left for me but to hope and pray for the bullet to end it all and soon. I no longer fraternize with the few men who remain in the unit. Anyone I get close to dies.

There is a red glow in the sky to the north. The jungle is on fire, miles away, but there is no sound. I do not think the silence can get any deeper. Then I feel a pull on the wire. My wrist jerks and I pull back to acknowledge I am awake. I pull on my ankle wire and get a similar response. I daren't look over the trench. I keep my mouth open and listen for any sound. Then I hear a faint clipping noise. I wait. If we fire too soon they will back off and come later. I want to get the attack over with, so I can get some sleep. I check my gun and pick up a grenade with my free hand. I never played cricket when I was a kid but I could throw stones and now that throwing arm comes in handy. I just need to time the first one. Throwing it about 25 yards I can get a good spread of shrapnel over a large area and anything standing gets hit. I keep my head down as the No. 36 grenade can detonate large fragments over 50 yards. Being quartermaster I made sure we all have more than enough grenades. Just throw them far enough and don't mess up on the four-second fuse.

I imagine the first wave of Japs crawling on their hands and knees very slowly towards my trench. I have seen what they have done to other gun emplacements and how they butchered fellow soldiers. Just as I pull the pin the wire jerks three times and I almost drop the grenade. I lose the pin in the dark. Now I have to throw it. I keep a grip on the spoon, but not for too long, as I do not trust the workmanship. It's made in Britain. I have seen what a grenade can do to the thrower. Then I remember the three tugs was a signal to get ready to fire. I cannot wait any longer. I give three pulls back and repeat the three on my leg wire.

Without showing my head over the trench I swing my arm back and throw the grenade as far and as high as I can. It explodes before it hits the ground. I could say all hell broke loose but we were already in hell. It just gets noisy. I put my gun over the top of the trench and give it a few bursts in my prescribed arc. I hear the Brens join in and more grenades explode. I throw another and take a quick peek after the explosion. I can see outlines of Japs near me, far too near and I can hear a Jap screaming what I now know to be "Banzai!" They are charging.

For the next few minutes I do not stop firing or throwing grenades. My magazine runs out and I throw more grenades before changing it. I lose track of time, magazines and grenades. Then it is all over. Nothing but screams and shouts in a language I cannot understand. So I throw a few more grenades. I think they are the last. I cannot find anymore in the crate. The screams and shouts stop.

I tug on the wrist wire and get no response. The foot wire is still alive. So I untie them and taking my Sten gun, crawl along the trench to where the nearest Bren gun emplacement is. There should have been two men there but all I can see are parts of bodies, an army helmet and the handle of a Jap sword embedded in something. Nothing else was distinguishable. There is a smell of blood, gunpowder and death. I would vomit if I had any food in me. Another two men lost and I didn't even know their names. Poor sods.

The rest of the night is quite. Amongst all the carnage, I never found the telephone or wires that connect to the Brigade H.Q. But two men crawl through our trench system to my position and replace the other two. One of them attaches the wire to his wrist and signals to me that they are ready to defend. I can hear the sounds of their Bren gun as they make it ready. We do not get rid of the bodies until well after dawn. Even in death, Jap soldiers can be booby-trapped and no one wants to touch them. Later that morning I collect another Samurai sword for my collection I keep in a truck back at the wagon lines.

TWO

I AM TOO TENSE to sleep or stand-down. I lie in my trench and can't risk another smoke. My thoughts drift back home. I long to hear from my wife, to know about the daughter I haven't seen yet and my son who will soon be going to school. Will I survive and see them again? We are starved of news and wonder about air raids and what the plans are for the second front and the Middle East.

I want to get out of this god forsaken bloody country and see our egotistical politicians go for weeks without a wash, unable to take a shit anywhere safe and sleep out without a groundsheet or blanket. There are the relentless biting insects, giant spiders and snakes not to mention either dust or rain and humidity. Then there are these suicidal attacks by wild screaming Japs, who want to kill you. But I cannot dwell on what I have no control over, so I dream about what it must be like at home. The jungle is quiet again. The stars are out. All I need is a decent cup of tea, a real bed and more than anything, my family.

I sat outside in the garden of our home in early June 1940, under the stars, the day before my son was born.

In early June 1940, when the evacuation of Dunkirk was in full swing, everyone living within a certain distance of the East coast or adjacent to the Rochford airfield, had been given 48 hours notice to evacuate. Most people had already moved away, but we decided to stay until after the baby was born. There had been a few sneak raids but, in general, it was reasonably quiet. Even the evacuation of the British Expeditionary Force from Dunkirk had not altered the atmosphere or shattered our peace, so far. We realized we would be compelled to move away soon as, being in a restricted area, essential services could not be guaranteed and we would not be able to have an air raid shelter installed. The airstrip runway, which ended just over the road in front of our bungalow, had been taken over by the Royal Air Force (R.A.F.) as an advance fighter base.

On the evening I arrived home from London, it was as if the whole world was asleep. The outside temperature was in the high eighties. My wife's pregnancy was at an advanced stage. She greeted me and I remarked on her sunburn. She had spent that day with one of our last remaining neighbors and had been sitting in the sun all day amongst the roses.

We had finished the evening meal and my wife complained of back-ache. We thought her fatigue was because of the heat. We sat in the garden and relaxed as the temperature cooled, watching our pet dog digging holes in the garden. There was no moon that night and the stars shone with an extra brilliance in the total blackout. Her back ache got worse but in our inexperience we restrained from calling our doctor, even if he was available, which we doubted, so we decided to take a walk. We commenced our walk toward the hospital. It was very eerie, complete silence and utter darkness, when her pains became more frequent. We tried to hurry and we eventually reached the hospital entrance. An attendant whisked my wife away and I was told to leave and report in the morning with her suitcase that we had omitted to bring. I walked home alone and, next day, on hearing the news that our son had been born, the war took on a new significance.

The date was June 6th 1940.

During the days that followed, troops arrived in our locality to occupy empty houses. Concrete bunkers were built adjacent to our bungalow and trenches dug in front gardens. There was feverish activity everywhere and the Rochford airstrip came to life as Hurricane fighter planes landed and took off. Bedraggled groups of soldiers marched past our bungalow, most of them without firearms. It became painfully obvious that we were unprepared for the threatened invasion. The outlook was very serious and we gave thanks to Winston Churchill for his gift of oratory, for his encouragement and determination to promote the powerful effort needed at that time. The day the baby arrived home we had an air raid and bombs fell close by and the continuous barrage of Ack-Ack gunfire (Anti-Aircraft) most of the night, made it impossible to sleep. Next morning my wife and baby went to London to stay with her relatives. I remained behind but moved to Aston Clinton, near Aylesbury in Buckinghamshire, with my firm, where, later, my wife and baby joined me. Here we enjoyed several tranquil weeks of happiness, as a family.

On the morning of October 15th 1940, I received a call at the office from my wife. She sounded rather disturbed. I had received an official envelope in the post that morning and it was my call up papers. I was directed to report for duty on the October 17th, which didn't give us much time. I left the office, never to return to my old desk again. My 30th birthday fell on October 2nd, and my employers thought I might still qualify for exemption. But, like most efforts in those first war years, it was half hearted. Added to which, most men left in the clerical department were older than me. In spite of the pleasant comradeship, it was 'blow you Jack, I'm all right'. I had been studying for my final Accountancy exams.

I was a very reluctant soldier, as I bid my wife and little son goodbye. I hitched a ride to London, then a train to Shoeburyness. I had no travel vouchers; the authorities had sent the papers to my old address in Rochford. The only train available made an extensive tour of Tilbury docks. I seemed to be on it for hours, and it was deserted. When the train finally arrived at Shoeburyness, only a handful of men alighted and I joined them on the platform. We were all dressed in dark business suits, carried suitcases, and looked as if we had arrived for a business conference. We walked slowly down the platform to the exit; no one was in much of a hurry to give up his freedom.

It was a beautiful day, the sun was warm and the long hot summer was not yet ready to give way to autumn. The general atmosphere reminded me of the holiday camp we once went to, everyone was so friendly. I wandered down the road, as directed, watching the vapor trails of fighter planes overhead, weaving and diving and wondered if there had been a recent air raid warning. I arrived at the entrance of the Royal Artillery Establishment. It was empty, and I began to wonder whether I had come to the right place. It was an impressive entrance, neat and tidy, not a blade of grass out of place, and unmistakable as it was signposted, so, I made my way down a long drive leading to the buildings I could see ahead. I had visualized squads of men training like mad for the war effort.

I walked slowly down the path to the main building, admiring the late summer flowerbeds. I was still on my own, apart from the few fighter planes buzzing around overhead.

The contents of the letter I received with the conscription papers, quoted something about taking sufficient clothing for the weekend, in a suitcase. I wondered if that bore any significance to the fact that the place was deserted. Perhaps, when they gave me a medical check up they would realize I was not the right type and was too underweight. I wore glasses so I would be of no use to them. They would take one look at me and send me home. On the other hand, perhaps I was a special case and that's why the place was deserted? I was meditating on this thought when, approaching a hole in the ground, which turned out to be the entrance to an underground air raid shelter, I was grabbed by a sergeant who forcibly directed me down a flight of steps into an air raid shelter.

"Git fell in darn their son, dew wanna git killed?"

Life at last.

I was directed to sit down on one of the long benches in this huge underground shelter and, when my eyes became accustomed to the semi darkness, I noticed other men, also in civvies and clutching weekend cases. We sat in silence and were not allowed to smoke. We looked mystified when told to sit to attention. Later that afternoon, as soon as the all clear had been sounded, we were marched away into the main barracks.

So began the routine of being processed and bedded down for the night. We were taken from place to place, accumulating a mountain of blankets, bedding, the regulation knife, fork and spoon, an enamel mug and a plate.

After an evening meal of sausages and baked beans, we were taken to what was to be our barracks and allocated a bed. Before we had time to settle down, we had a visit from a man, of smallish stature, who seemed very friendly at first. For some unexplainable reason I have rarely liked or trusted small men and I took an instant dislike to this chap. The first thing he did was to draw attention to his two stripes and that, when addressing him, we must stand to attention and address him as bombardier. He boasted that he was the bastard of the Regiment and if we persisted in taking the piss out of him with our dumb insolence, he would take the shit out of us when he called us to parade at six a.m. the following Monday morning.

During the next 48 hours we did not have a moments peace.

We were inoculated, documented several times, kitted out, and had a medical inspection, dressed in our comic ill fitting uniforms, and nursed the wounds where we had been punctured several times. Eight men had been allocated to our room, each having a bed and locker. We lost no time introducing ourselves and getting to know each other, and so began an association of men who became comrades in arms in the months to come.

THREE

THE FOLLOWING MONDAY morning, before 6 a.m., we were ready for that first parade, sitting on our beds, in the dark, having lined up to wash and shave in cold water, in the dark, of course. We dressed as best we could in our ill-fitting uniforms and this set the pattern for the next four weeks.

There were twenty-four men in our squad.

I regretted not participating in any kind of sport in my teens. I had thought I was reasonably fit for my age but the constant drilling was punishment. We all had aching limbs and sore feet and were in a state of collapse each night. We all agreed that this would pass if we accepted this humiliation without complaint. We had no alternative. We spent the time between the evening meal and lights out nursing blistered feet. We learned how to soak our army boots in buckets of water whilst wearing several pairs of socks, risking punishment if discovered. We wrote home to our folks telling them how much we were enjoying ourselves.

When a group of men are confined together, night and day, time will tend to group them according to their mentality, like to like, and I was fortunate in the comradeship of some who would travel with me to India and Burma, and most would not return.

One was Johnny Griffin, with whom I had an instant rapport. He was a Londoner and had recently married so had not yet started a family. He showed a great interest in my small son and often talked of the family he and his wife planned after the war.

It was natural that we spent the little spare time we had together. A card game with a gamble was something we both enjoyed, whilst indulging in blasphemous moans as we nursed our aching limbs. We, the new recruits of 'A' battery, devoted the entire hours of daylight to drill on the parade ground, wet or fine, and were expected to cram three years of normal peace time training into three months.

Automatic drilling soon became a bore as every move we made was accompanied by a shout. We shouted left-right-left-right, repeating the maneuver over and over again, by numbers, until we became proficient. The louder we shouted, the more proficient we seemed to become, and, in three weeks we could complete a whole drill routine faultlessly and in complete silence.

To succumb to authority was our greatest endurance, as the task of our instructors appeared to be to break our spirit. It is an Army boast that they could do with us exactly as they wanted, which of course they did. They told us the only thing they couldn't do was to put us in the family way, but they would even try this, if necessary. We had to suffer in silence when that bastard of a bombardier had us marking time in muddy fields or flooded parade grounds, just to satisfy his ego, and to keep us busy during the evenings cleaning up to be ready for early morning inspection. He had the infuriating habit of standing in front of one, within a few inches and looking up into one's face and shouting. Being small, he was compelled to look up to us. Woe to anyone who looked down at him. Several squads in 'A' Battery drilled at the same time creating a din, which was confusing to say the least, resulting in some humorous incidents.

Wednesday afternoons were set aside for recreational training and invariably, this consisted of a route march or cross-country run.

As we had to parade at the bath house for the weekly ablutions after the Wednesday afternoon exertions, it was arranged that the squads returned from their run or march at staggered intervals so that the showers were not over crowded. Bath parade was compulsory. Trouble was that those last in the shower had cold water.

In our room we swore never to volunteer for anything, under any circumstances, and the incident on the first recreational parade proved our wisdom. We were all dressed in P.T. shorts, singlets and army boots, ready for the run or march, whichever was decided upon. After inspection at close quarters, our bombardier, who breathed scented cashews into our faces, whilst we looked straight ahead, asked if anyone could drive a car, told us all to shut up and then talked of something else. He then said.

"When I give the command I want all those who can drive to step one pace forward in the front row, and one step backward, in the back row." He then gave the command.

"Squad, squad, shon! Volunteers one step outward March!"

Eight men stepped out of line and he took their names and numbers and instructed them to dress for inspection, just as soon as they had completed their ablutions, after the cross-country run. They really thought they were on to something good, but six were detailed for the cookhouse until lights out and the other two were given the task of cleaning the bombardier's bicycle.

After about two weeks of continuous foot and rifle drill, our instructor developed a sore throat so, on the pretence of looking for suitable men to be put forward for promotion, we were all given the task of drilling the squad. We found ourselves imitating the bombardier, with his loud and crisp commands. George McWilliams was by far the best, but no one got promoted. George was born in Liverpool, and spoke in a broad Lancashire accent, with a strong gruff voice. His speech always began with a conjunction. It was always, fooking this or fooking that and he could never make up his mind on anything. He wasn't married and had wealthy parents who had tried, unsuccessfully, to get him a commission.

Every morning, including Saturdays, we paraded for P. T. in shorts and singlets and the sergeant instructors demonstrated physical feats that we were expected to perform. I had never seen an exercise horse at close quarters before, but had to try everything the others attempted. The first time I took a running jump over the horse, I nearly broke my neck. It was a long time before I became enthusiastic and proficient. After a month in 'A' battery, we were given forty-eight hours leave.

We were now veterans and transferred to 'B' Battery. The atmosphere was friendlier and we were able to gloat as we viewed the new recruits on the other side of the road separating the two batteries. Most of our time was now spent at lectures and we were taught the rudiments of gunnery. This was a relief from the constant routine of parades and drilling. We were not allowed to relax for fear of failing examinations and the threat of transfer to an infantry unit.

At about 4 a.m. one morning, our sergeant burst into our room and had us out of bed and standing to attention. It was early December and very cold, and we were given two minutes to dress and parade outside in the black out. There was an invasion scare and we were going to be front line troops. They called this exercise the 'Lawn line'. We stumbled around in the dark, collected webbing equipment, a Lee Enfield .303 rifle and bayonet, with ten rounds of ammunition and, with the sergeant's help, assembled all this junk together. The rifles were covered in grease. We were then transported to Shoeburyness marshes where we marched over muddy fields to a pillbox that smelled of rotting vegetables and animal droppings. It was very dark. We sat on the cement floor, still half asleep, and, one by one went outside to urinate. There were only ten of us here and we couldn't hear or see a thing. The humor of our situation soon became apparent as we whispered our thoughts, accompanied by farts from outside. We had no idea who was supposed to be in charge; none of us had ever fired a rifle before. The presence of so much grease discouraged us from wanting to fire it.

It wasn't long before we decided to smoke and to keep a look out for our senior Non Commissioned Officer (N.C.O.). The enemy wouldn't have had much trouble from us. Much later that morning, we were taken back for a late breakfast and were told the invasion scare was a false alarm but, some time later, bodies of German troops were washed up around that coast. It would have been easy for the Germans to have invaded then.

We were confined to barracks and no one ever managed to get a pass, so we found a way to get out without being discovered, and, in turn, planned to take unofficial leave. I left the barracks late one Friday afternoon, took a bus into Southend, caught a train to Stratford, changed to the underground and made my way home to Aston Clinton, mostly without tickets and flashing a piece of paper that looked like a travel warrant. I found it easy to dodge the military police by carrying a kit bag and making it appear that I was on official leave. During that weekend the City of London was bombed in one of the heaviest raids of the war, and on my way back to Shoeburyness, I became lost in the City I thought I was familiar with. Main thoroughfares were blocked with rubble from demolished buildings and every building was on fire. Entangled fire hoses and ankle deep water impeded progress through most streets. I helped with rescue operations along with other troops for the rest of the day. Here I met a gunner I recognized from my unit, so we kept together, and as soon as the opportunity presented itself, we made our way to Fenchurch Street station, only to find it closed and burned out. It too had been bombed.

Liverpool Street station was crowded with troops all waiting to get back to their units. The Salvation Army, working all night, provided refreshments, and the railway authorities put on a special train that took us back to Shoeburyness, via Chelmsford, just in time for roll call and breakfast.

The Battle of Britain had come and gone. London had been bombed and I had crawled amongst the rubble. But I had never seen a bomb fall from a plane, until one Thursday afternoon. It was late December and I was on guard duty at the time. The guard post was stationed at the entrance to the barracks near the officer's mess.

The sentry box was surrounded by sand bags, chest high and I marched up and down a small length of pathway, marked by two white lines, standing smartly to attention to salute everyone with pips on his shoulder. The traffic in officers was heavy.

I had just got warm, marching up and down, and was standing 'at ease' inside the sentry box, sheltered from the cold wind and watching the thousand or more men on pay parade about a hundred yards away. A pencil thin Heinkel He 117 bomber appeared flying low, silently gliding over the roof of the main barrack building. In that split second of recognition, there was no panic, I was more concerned to be ready to shoulder arms and salute the officer I saw coming along the path, than to blow my whistle. There was no sound. I couldn't believe this was an air raid but when I saw the swastika on the plane's wings, I thought it was in trouble and was about to make a forced landing. It was my duty to blow the whistle three times, in the event of a raid. I watched the plane release five bombs. This caught me by surprise, but I blew the whistle as hard as I could.

The parade ground cleared quickly.

The bombs looked like they were falling in a straight line towards me. I dived behind the sand bags for protection. The first two bombs exploded in soft earth on the boundary of the parade ground, the other two exploded near me. I was showered with clods of wet earth and stones. A large bomb buried itself in a muddy pool at the side of the path and did not explode. I quickly became the centre of interest, so I dropped all pretense of drill, as officers approached me. Most seemed to regard the whole affair as a bore and it was suggested I was a liar when I gave my version of the unexploded bomb. I was glad when my stint of duty came to an end. Next morning there was an official enquiry and I was convinced the officer who took my statement didn't believe me. Exactly one week later, at the same time of day, in the middle of pay parade, I was about to receive my money from the very officer who had called me a liar. The unexploded bomb went off.

The ground shook, there was a loud explosion and the contents of the muddy pool shot a hundred feet into the air and fell lazily across the parade ground before anyone realized what was happening. The officers sitting at the pay table didn't move and were covered with mud. The disbelieving officer's hat and uniform was coated in thick mud. He glared at me, furious. I stood to attention and tried not to laugh.

During the latter stages of our training program we had written tests in various subjects, and I made sure I wasn't a Signaler, as this entailed athletic prowess, but I was to the fore in anything to do with gunnery. At a later date, I discovered I was considered to be the best gun layer in the battery. When our training program came to an end we had an official seven days leave and were then ready for posting to an active service unit.

FOUR

IT WAS COLD and dark on a February afternoon in 1941 when our contingent of 240 men alighted at Hitchin railway station. The old market town, on the northern boundary of Hertfordshire, had a neglected and unfriendly appearance in the rain. It was far enough away to escape the bombing in London. Several schools had evacuated to the West Country. This made accommodation available for large numbers of troops and for those poor sods unfortunate enough to have been bombed out of their London homes. It was also a reception area for the less seriously sick and injured, thus releasing scarce hospital accommodation. Pregnant women paraded the streets, in pairs. There were also a large number of men of the Royal Artillery; in fact, the town was an army transit camp.

We marched from the railway station to an old building that was at one time a meat storage and slaughter warehouse and there was barely sufficient room for our contingent. The marble topped benches were used as bed space and many men had to sleep on the old wooden floor that was rotten and collapsed under pressure. Rats were a problem at night. This was our first taste of sleeping rough and we were not happy. We were at the strength of an anti-tank regiment. The army was billeted everywhere, in schools, church halls and commandeered houses. Parades were necessary for everything. We were confined to the old warehouse. Meals were provided in an old church hall about half a mile away and we marched, three times a day, down the street with mess tins, knife fork and spoon at the ready. These parades took place at fixed times, irrespective of the weather and sometimes we were made to dress in battle order with full packs, steel helmets and gas masks. We were not allowed to get slack; our new sergeant major and other senior N.C.O.s seemed to delight in disciplining us constantly.

Route marches were arranged whenever they could be fitted in and once a week we paraded and marched to the local baths for a hot bath and change of clothing. Facilities in the old warehouse were most inadequate, with a few outside toilets and taps to wash as best we could. On our first Sunday, the announcement of a compulsory parade prevented us from getting away for the weekend. Several hundred men were involved in this parade and we marched behind a full army band to church. After the degradation of the past few weeks we found this very uplifting. Only about a third of the parade were able to get into the church, the remainder, including our contingent, were marched up a side street nearby and dismissed. We had no idea, at the time, that this was to be a church parade otherwise most of us would have been off for the day and to hell with the consequences. This was the first and last of such parades and I have never had the pleasure of marching to an army band again.

Muster parades were held on weekends, thus preventing unofficial leave taking. The parades began outside the warehouse and the roll called. We were then marched to an open space where the main muster took place. We were convinced that most of these parades were organized for the benefit of a few top Brass, to show them how many men they had to play with. One such parade took place on a cold Sunday morning in March, when about seven thousand men were detailed for an overseas draft, to be sent to the Middle East. We learned later, that these men went to Crete. The men were taken in alphabetical order and marched away in groups, given a medical, documented and given leave passes for embarkation leave. They had all left the town by evening. Apparently some 300 men were rejected from this draft for some reason or other, (one, Lofty

Smith, because he was too tall) so that a further 300 men had to be found to make up the number.

When these men were chosen, next morning, Johnny and I with Taffy and Tom were on 24 hour guard duty, which was lucky for us, otherwise we may have suffered the same fate as those thousands of poor sods who went to Crete. A few days later, six of us were detailed to parade at a school hall that eventually became a quartermaster's store. Here, we helped to issue tropical kit to the men destined for Crete. The task lasted nearly three weeks. We were kept very busy and worked long hours until, quite suddenly, all the men had gone and the town was empty.

Unaware at the time of how it would affect my future with the unit, I used a typewriter during the stores duties and I am sure it was because of this that I was detailed to report to the battery office when the stores job came to an end.

After an early breakfast, we paraded at our usual place at 8.a.m., dressed for a route march with respirators, side packs and water bottles full. Our new bombardier called us to attention. The new R. S. (Royal Sergeant) arrived. We were ordered to order march for inspection by the Regimental Sergeant Major (R.S.M.). When he was directly behind me he tapped me on the shoulder and said, "Is your name Spill?"

"Yes Sir."

"Fall out and report to the office." He said.

So I fell out and marched off.

I was not sad to see my colleagues being marched off on the route march. It started to rain. That day, the lads suffered the longest march of all and covered nearly thirty miles.

The office was in a requisitioned house and the only furnishings were trestle tables and folding chairs, with a small safe in the room at the front. Kitchen cupboards and drawers were used for storage of army forms. My duties were the typing of daily orders and correspondence, hand written by the Commanding Officer (C.O.) and sometimes notes from other officers, the keeping of nominal rolls and making it appear that I was busy.

Almost every day there were new postings of men to and from the unit and the paper work kept me busy. On my second day at this job, the C.O. explained that our unit was the nucleus of a medium artillery regiment and that we would probably be shipped out to the Far East somewhere, and he impressed on me that anything I heard in the office should be considered top secret. This meant I was now on the permanent office staff and if we were going to be here for a long time, I determined to make the most of it.

It soon became obvious that we would have to wait for a boat and as there was a shortage of equipment we were going to be in Hitchin for a long time. But anything can happen in the army. So, having mastered the job, my main concern was to get as much leave as possible. I was very fortunate. I only worked office hours and finished at four p.m. on Fridays, until the following Monday morning. Early every Friday afternoon, the R.S.M and all the officers, except the duty officer, disappeared for the weekend. I was excused all parades and I usually knew what was going to occur two or three days in advance. I had to learn something about King's Regulations, the only copy of which was kept in the small office safe in the C.O.'s office, so I was given a duplicate key to the safe and took charge of the leave passes and travel vouchers.

My wife had moved to Reading to live with relatives and I was able to make the journey on several weekends, sometimes officially. But I never liked Reading and my wife was not happy there either, even though my sister was kind and considerate. The attitude of the local populace contributed to our unfavorable opinion of the town. The locals seemed to act as if the war was nothing to do with them. There, local shops were always crowded and there seemed to be plenty of people lounging around who should have been in the services or working for a living. This was a different world to London. Reading had not yet been bombed.

My blood pressure rose one day when two fashionably dressed young ladies attempted to shoulder push me into the gutter and remarked for my benefit that it was about time these lazy good for nothing soldiers did some fighting and should not be allowed on the streets. Most British people are very conservative and reticent but one day an incident occurred that was so amusing, I don't think I'll ever forget it.

I was on my way to see my wife and took a bus from the railway station to Caversham where they were living. The bus was full with about a dozen standing passengers downstairs. I had just offered my seat to an elderly lady, when the bus made a right hand turn to Caversham. Standing next to me was a female in her mid-twenties, fashionably dressed, and carrying a small dog, which was almost concealed in her furs. She pulled the cord several times in quick succession, the signal for the driver to make an emergency stop. He slammed on the brakes. The sudden jolt sent most of the standing passengers cascading up to the front of the bus and some finished up on the floor. The young woman in furs fell on top of me with her dog breathing in my face. No one said anything until the bus conductor enquired as to who had wrung the bell. Adapting a haughty manner and standing as high as her extra high heels would permit, the young lady said.

"I did."

"Why?" Asked the bus conductor adding, "You might have caused some injury directing the driver to make an emergency stop like that?"

"But I asked for Caversham Heights and the driver has taken the wrong turning." Said the young lady.

"I'm sorry miss, we only go to Caversham. Caversham Heights is the other way and you will have to get off." Said the conductor.

This time all the passengers were silent and listening.

"But can't you see I come from the Heights?" Exclaimed the lady in a very superior voice.

I could not contain myself any longer and roared with laughter. The whole bus was in an uproar as the lady from the Heights left the bus. I hadn't heard anything so funny for ages and a miracle occurred as passengers began to speak to each other.

In contrast to the prolonged sunshine of 1940 we now suffered the drabness of 1941. It hadn't stopped raining since last winter and during this long wet period, anxiety as to our future persisted but, at last, orders arrived detailing embarkation procedure.

We were all given ten days embarkation leave.

It was 22nd June 1941 and Hitler had just launched his fatal invasion on the Soviet Union.

My wife had moved again to live with a sister in London. I was expected to sail almost immediately, but the days dragged on and nothing happened. We were on twenty-four hour standby so I dared not take liberties with unofficial leave.

One Saturday, I persuaded my wife to visit me. She caught an early morning coach and I knew the number 13 bus left the town at the early hour of 3.45.p.m. That would only give us a short time together. Also, that morning, I had heard we would be traveling up to Scotland on the following Friday, where a boat would be waiting. But I couldn't tell her or anyone else for that matter as I was sworn to secrecy. So, just in case, I made enquiries and the R.S.M. gave me the name and address of a lady who had accommodation to spare and I booked a room for the Saturday night.

My wife was pregnant again and I didn't want her harassed, also I knew my small son would be well taken care of. This would be our last meeting for a very long time, in fact, we didn't know if, or when, we would see each other again. We met at the bus stop, found a cafe and had lunch.

Time went fast. We walked and talked and we both knew the last bus had left for London, long before we got to the bus stop.

"Darling, I think I know someone who may be able to put us up for the night, then you could get the bus tomorrow. Hope your sister will guess what's happened." I said.

So we went along to see the lady I had already booked a room with and rang the front door bell.

"I hope she can put us up," I said, but I should have kept my mouth shut. The front door opened and the lady said.

"Hello Mr. Spill. Your room is ready, will you come in?"

My embarrassment was dispelled when we were invited to share this woman's mere rations that helped contribute to my leave. The memory of this weekend gave me the courage to withstand many hardships and kept my faith that we would eventually be together again.

The following Monday morning, at a muster parade, held in the temporary dining hall, the Medical Officer (M.O.) talked on the subject of health in the tropics and what we should expect, such things as wearing a hat during the heat of day, boiling all drinking water and the purchase of food from bazaars. He went on to say.

"The tension and excitement of the present environment encroaches on our normal pattern of life and creates adrenalin which is often put to misuse. We tend to be promiscuous, as is evidenced by the large number of unmarried young girls you see roaming the streets of this town, all in the family way. Very few of these girls will get married during hostilities but I want to warn you men of the dangers of V.D. This is rampant in the Far East. I warn you chaps, it's a crime in the army to contract V.D. and punishments are severe. A large number of local girls have been found to have V.D. and if any of you have had contact with them, you are advised to see the medical orderly next door, at any time. He will assist you. I would advise you to soak your genitals in a strong solution of permanganate of potash which is freely available, or report sick if you think you have any symptom of disease."

We were kept busy during the next few days updating medical injections and collecting tropical kit.

On Friday morning the M.O. held a medical inspection. We were to entrain for the boat later that day, but no one was aware of this at the time. This was a muster parade and there were no excuses for absenteeism. We paraded in the dining room, naked to the waist, ready to drop our slacks when ordered. I had charge of the nominal roll. It was estimated that at least half the men had large brown stains around their private parts and this caused great amusement. As soon as the parade was over, orders were received to move. We marched, with kit bags slung across our shoulders and in full marching order, to the railway station.

It was ten o'clock at night when the train steamed out in the rain. The journey was broken only once, at York for refreshments, and, early next morning the train was shunted over railway sidings and on to the dock, up to the side of a waiting ship.

FIVE

IT WAS VERY cold as we paraded prior to boarding the ship. The fog did not hide the two massive funnels of this huge passenger liner. This grey monster, the Windsor Castle, 660 feet long and 19,000 tons, would be our home for the next few weeks. If only I had had the opportunity to take a cruise on her in peacetime. The silence was uncanny as, in single file, we mounted the gangway and were herded out of the drizzle, like sheep entering an abattoir, then absorbed into various parts of the ship. I found it difficult to overcome the feeling of foreboding, as the deck began to rise and fall. The knowledge that I was now part of a huge war machine overwhelmed me. There was no escape. I would be fed, pushed to and fro, to satisfy the whims of the so-called experts. My opinion would never be asked for and I now realized, too late, that I was now an army number and a statistic, rather than a person. Things would happen now over which I had no control. How incredibly stupid we were to allow ourselves to be caught up in this militant fervor.

One hundred and twenty of us were crowded into a room at the stern, just below the water line. Our first instruction was to remove our boots. Only P. T. plimsoles were allowed to be worn during the voyage. All our kit was stacked against the bulkhead wall on the ship's side and the camber held everything in place, on the opposite side, bedding had been neatly stacked and we were ordered to sit on the long forms at the tables that were affixed to the deck and occupied half the deck space. The cabin would be kept clear during meals and inspected every morning, when tables and decks would be scrubbed clean. Here we would sleep and eat, and, as there was insufficient bed space to sleep everyone at the same time, some of us would be on guard duties to ease the position. Duties would be on a roster system.

That night, mattresses covered all available floor space, including on and under the tables, whilst hammocks were slung from hooks in the low ceiling. I preferred a hammock and soon mastered the art of swinging myself up. Johnny swung his hammock next to me and this was considered to be our domain for the remainder of the voyage. We had no portholes, but could feel the movement of the ship and the constant throb of the engines had a therapeutic quality that, added to our close proximity, gave us a sense of security. Despite the lack of sleep on the train journey we had a realistic feeling of excitement at the prospect of danger, and this inhibited sleep.

The ship was not designed to carry such a large contingent and we were hampered by a shortage of toilet and washing facilities and often plagued by blocked latrines and flooded gangways. We soon discovered that the best parts of the ship were occupied by R.A.F. personnel, including all the cabins. They outnumbered us by about six to one.

There was a twenty-four hour guard at strategic places in the ship well below the water line and next to watertight doors, which had to be securely closed during boat drill. Those on guard duty, who were not on station, were required on the upper decks stationed at selected positions near lifeboats, to maintain order in the event of an emergency. The guard was issued with .303 Lee Enfield rifles and ten rounds of ammunition and I wondered when we would be called upon to use them. Those on guard were supposed to be the last to leave the ship.

Lifeboat drill kept us busy during those first few days.

Our boat station was on the top deck and entailed negotiating various passages, steep stairways and ladders and this we did several times a day, each time fully dressed and in our greatcoats, as it was very cold outside.

Ship life soon became routine, frequent fatigues and men detailed to other parts of the ship for duty made room for those remaining.

On the fourth day out, the sea began to cut up rough and the strong wind rocked the ship that began to rise and fall to an alarming degree. Seasickness now became prevalent making the fresh air on deck preferable to the stench below, but it was bitterly cold. Several of us leaned on the ship's rail watching the water rise and fall, the sea dark and menacing when, a crewmember that was with us, suggested that we were in for a storm.

The convoy presented an impressive sight with seventeen massive cruise liners, now converted into troop ships, plus five large supply ships, a dozen destroyers in line, side by side, spread out at the head of the convoy, an aircraft carrier and a cruiser in attendance. We only saw the cruiser once when we had a fleeting glimpse of it through the fog. As we watched, the whole convoy turned to port and the destroyers were then on the starboard side. When the ship gave a lurch as a large wave hit us, we got drenched so, reluctantly, we made our way below.

That afternoon the predicted storm arrived and continued for the following forty-eight hours. The ship was thrown about like a cork and I was thankful for my hammock, as those on mattresses slid off the tables and across the polished floor. We lost a great deal of crockery and food was wasted in more ways than one. Twice, during the storm we had lifeboat drills. Once during the night and this gave us something to moan about, as it was very difficult to keep one's footing, let alone climb the steep stairways and steel ladders. During the fifth day at sea the storm abated and the ship settled down to a routine roll, whilst the pounding waves sent shudders through the superstructure. Later that afternoon other noises confirmed that depth charges were being dropped and at one time a destroyer passed us at high speed and was so close that we thought our cabin walls would cave in under the pressure of the explosions.

It was some time after lights out that there was a deafening explosion. The ship lurched, my hammock swung steeply as my hips hit the ceiling, first to one side then the other, but I hung on. Many men fell from their hammocks on to those sleeping below whilst those on the floor became mixed up in a heap at one end of the deck. We thought the ship was about to turn over when, suddenly, all the lights were switched on and warning bells began to ring, as the ship rolled violently from side to side. We grabbed our clothes and arrived at our allocated boat stations in record time after negotiating the stairs and ladders half dressed and carrying what we could. Watertight doors were closed behind us. But there was no panic. The blackout was ignored and all the ship's lights were on but we couldn't see much because of the fog. A white shroud that we hoped would give some protection surrounded us.

It was an eerie feeling, as if this was the end of our world. The ship's engines had stopped and there was a frightening list to starboard making it difficult to stand upright. Warning bells rang in the distance. Our boat station was on the starboard side of the ship, and as it rolled, it was as if we would quietly slip into the sea. It was a long way down to the water from the top deck. The reflection of the ship's lights against the fog, made it difficult to distinguish anything. We stood there in silence shivering and not knowing what to expect and the cold penetrated all our clothing, adding to our fears.

We noticed the lifeboat adjacent to our boat station was missing and news from other parts of the deck suggested that several of the lifeboats had gone from the starboard side. The ship appeared to be sinking and we all knew we did not stand a chance of survival without lifeboats. We would soon freeze to death in the sea.

We waited for some time, listening, before anyone spoke, even then only in a whisper. The white fog enveloped us. Johnny was the first to speak, he whispered.

"What I would like to know is, how the hell can they launch the boats from the port side with this list?"

There was no answer to that.

"Stop fooking pushing!" Exclaimed the man directly in front of me.

I recognized his voice even though he was smothered under several scarves. It was George McWilliams.

"What do you recken, George?" I whispered.

"If they fooking thought the boat was fooking sinking we would hear destroyers nearby, but I haven't heard a fooking thing so that's a good sign unless, of cos, it's another fook up. They say half the fooking bridge is missing."

Surely the Navy wouldn't desert us now? There were more than fifteen hundred men standing about on deck wondering whether this was their last hours in this world.

As time went on there was a great deal of argument around us as to what had occurred and what should happen next, until we heard someone shout.

"Fucking balls up!"

Which proved that, even in moments of adversity there could still be humor. So, one by one, we sat on the deck and lit cigarettes. We had all brought plenty with us.

Several cigarettes later, and near to midnight, someone remembered to turn the warning bells off. The noise was getting on our nerves and any U-boat in the vicinity would have got the message by now. It was extremely cold and rivulets of ice had formed where men had pissed on the deck. A squeal from the P. A. system warned that an announcement was about to be made.

"Attention please. We do not know at this stage how serious the damage is, we have been holed below the water line near the bridge, but the prompt action of the guards and crew, in closing the watertight doors has prevented serious flooding. It is hoped to have the pumps working shortly, meantime, we are asking for volunteers to help bring up material from below decks to construct extra rafts. Will those volunteers report to the officer on the poop deck please, meantime, the remainder of you stay at your boat stations. Out!"

There was a stampede as our group made a dash for it. We couldn't get down to the poop deck quick enough. Anything was better than sitting around in the cold doing nothing.

We thought Lofty Smith was going to be our first casualty when he knocked himself out. One of the crew had found some heavy pieces of timber in a hold, well below the water line and we were working in about a foot of water that had seeped into the hold when Lofty, standing up too quickly in a steel doorway, hit the top of his head on the doorframe and collapsed into the water.

It was no easy job to get him up the narrow steel ladders to the upper decks; he was about six feet six inches tall, and heavy. Later, when we talked to a crew member, he confided that he was one of the ship's engineers and that, if they got the ship underway again, they would need a gun crew. There was a gun mounted on the stern that had never been used. There had been some loss of life when watertight doors were closed but we never found out the extent of the casualties or, for that matter, what caused the incident.

At daybreak it was announced the ship's pumps were working, that it would be some time before a further announcement would be made, meantime, everyone was ordered below for breakfast, then to stand by for further orders. The main convoy didn't wait for us, we were on our own and very vulnerable to U-boat attack, and, for this reason there was feverish activity bringing up on to the main deck anything that would float, to be used as life rafts. At about three p.m., we could feel the throb of the ship's engines as they were started up and, as the ship began to move we all cheered. There had been much activity all day, cargo had been moved, some things thrown overboard, and compartments flooded so that the ship was now on a more even keel, but the list to starboard was still pronounced and caused concern.

The ship moved along in a calm sea at about five knots, and in the slight swell an orange sun shone through the fog, during the late afternoon. On one occasion we were sure we saw icebergs and it was extremely cold. There was no lack of volunteers for submarine lookout from now on. A school of whales, thought at first to be U-boats, was sighted one morning and this caused a panic. We all became navigators, and if our calculations proved accurate, we would soon land in Newfoundland, as we sailed west for the next few days. There was no sign of the convoy. We could be going to Canada or the U.S.A. for repairs, as we couldn't possibly continue the journey with such a pronounced list.

Lofty had been taken up to the sick bay, suffering, we were told, from concussion. We had just had our midday meal and George, Tom, Johnny and I had settled down to a game of cards for the afternoon on the floor of the cabin. Taffy, who was usually our fourth, was on duty roster.

Tom Short was a five foot four package of muscle and brawn. When we complained of physical exhaustion he, in turn, would boast he wasn't getting enough exercise. He had a small farm in Norfolk that he inherited from his father. He knew no other life but farming, was married, had two children, both at school. He could never understand why he had been called up and hoped his wife would be able to pull strings and get him out of the army to save the farm from ruin. He rolled his own cigarettes and smoked the most atrocious tobacco.

Later, Taffy joined us and expressed his concern for Lofty saying.

"I think I'll go along to see Lofty and see what I can find out."

We regarded Taffy Jones as a con man. He was gifted with that rare Welsh cunning. In Civvy Street he was a sales rep, but he was reluctant to speak of himself or his family.

We had been playing cards for some time before Taffy returned and sat himself down on the floor beside us. He waited until Tom completed a successful hand of abundance.

"Well?" asked Tom.

"You wouldn't believe it," said Taffy. "Here am I, comfortable on Lofty's bed, who by the way is alright now, when in marches that chap we saw down below, you know, the ship's engineer, the one that mentioned something about the six-inch gun mounted on the stern? Remember? Right, now then, where was I? Ah yes, the gun. Did you know some of the gun crew were drowned, the night we were hit? Well, it appears they can't raise a gun team amongst the crew now and I've told this chap he needn't worry, as we would take on the job, we have had experience with six-inch naval guns and he seemed impressed. And guess what? I gave him our six names and he is going to see the ship's captain and our own officer to see what he can arrange."

"Do you think he will do that?" I asked.

"And what about the rest of our chaps, will they also be considered?" asked Johnny.

"No. I think this man is genuine and he wants a permanent crew so he won't mess around."

Answered Taffy, " I tell you what, if we had been hit a few seconds earlier, the lot of us wouldn't be here now, our cabin would have been flooded".

Next day, all six of us were detailed to parade at the stern of the ship. Lofty joined us even though he had been excused duties for seven days. Several officers were present, including the ship's officers and the gun was uncovered. We were told we were privileged, as this was the first time the gun had been uncovered since it was fitted and tested. After inspection, we gave a demonstration gun drill and we got the job, thanks to the audacity of Taffy. We were now a permanent gun crew for the remainder of the voyage and this excused us from all other duties. The ship's engineer confided that he hoped it would never be necessary to fire the gun, as the ship would probably break in two in view of the hole in her side. Meantime, the ship changed course and sailed south, skirting Bermuda and constantly zigzagging. The decks were always crowded as we were all ardent submarine lookouts. It was warmer on deck now, and despite the list to starboard, most of us crowded on the port side, hoping it would help. Sitting on deck, one could see only the sky on one side and the sea on the other.

SIX

EARLY ONE MORNING, we were aware that the ship was not moving and the engines had stopped. We had dropped anchor at Freetown in Sierra Leone. Looking out from the port side we were surprised to see how near we were to the shore. The natives were jet black and sat on their haunches and watched us as we watched them, in silence. We could see into the native huts and noticed the children were nude. The heavy showers, which came from a cloudless sky, soaked us quickly and it was very hot and humid.

Soon, native canoes arrived manned by small boys who looked just about old enough to go to school and they were naked. They shouted up to us for 'Liverpool shillings' or 'Glasgow Tanners' and, when we responded, they dived into the muddy waters and disappeared whilst their canoes drifted away on the fast flowing tide. We wondered whether they would ever recover them and were relieved to see them surface and climb into their canoes a hundred yards away. We ran out of shillings and six-pences and threw down farthings covered in tin foil from cigarette packets and the little boys called out.

"Hey mister, you fuck me up!"

We were not the first troops to call there. Soon, many larger native boats arrived and we watched as the natives paddled, keeping abreast and fighting the strong tide. Those in the larger boats now threw up ropes with hooks attached that enabled us to haul up baskets of local produce and there was much shouting and bargaining. Bananas were a penny a dozen which was all we bought, coconuts we used as missiles. Many official launches came and went and we longed to be on the move again as it was so hot. There were several other ships at anchor within sight but no sign of any of our convoy.

That night we quietly slipped out of sight of land and cruised down the coast to Cape Town. We fraternized with the R.A.F. as we sailed down the west coast of Africa, enjoyed a crossing of the line ceremony, had several concerts arranged by the R.A.F. and formed various card schools. P.T. on deck before breakfast was exhilarating and the weather glorious, enabling us to sunbathe on our private deck beside the gun. It was now warm enough to sleep on deck under the stars, and the incredible contrast of this part of our journey did much to lighten our spirits.

A highlight of the cruise were the boxing matches.

One of our gunners was lightweight boxing champion of Liverpool. He spent all his time training below decks, even through the heat of the day. He won all his events during the first contests on the main deck, all under army rules. Later, it was arranged that he fought the heavyweight boxing champion of the R.A.F. over fifteen rounds and we had plenty of side bets. Our gunner couldn't go wrong and knocked out his opponent in the thirteenth round. This little chap never mixed with the others and was reluctant to go ashore at Cape Town, but, when he did finally go, he didn't come back, and we never learned what happened to him.

Table Mountain was a heavenly sight, after being at sea for seven weeks. The huge Cape rollers tossed the ship about like a cork and when riding on the crest of a wave we had a glimpse of Cape Town sparkling in the sunshine, new and white, unlike any other city. The Windsor Castle would be in dry dock for two or three weeks and it was arranged for us to go ashore every day, when not on duty, from mid-day until one thirty a.m. the following morning. Our the gun team could go ashore every day, if we wished.

The main convoy had called into Cape Town and sailed a month earlier and ours was the only troop ship in dock, so we had the town to ourselves.

We were not allowed ashore until the second day, when there was a muster parade and we were all taken on a route march around the town. From that day onwards and for the remainder of our stay we went ashore every day. The civil authorities had obviously had a great deal of experience at entertaining troops and the local woman's guild and other organizations spared no expense on our behalf. Waiting for us each day, just outside the dock gates, were dozens of cars, two females per car, anxious to entertain us. We were only allowed ashore in pairs, after inspection. These women took us to their homes, gave us fabulous meals, and took us to cinemas and theatres and trips around the town. We were impressed by the high living standards and the incredible comparison with living in Britain at that time. I made several visits to the top of Table Mountain by cable car. We drew lots everyday to see who would meet the same women twice. The whites all seemed to have large white painted houses with huge gardens, many black servants and large American cars. We couldn't tell the difference between a white and a Cape colored as their color was the same but they lived in different areas, as did the blacks.

On one occasion we were taken to the quarters of the town reserved for the blacks and were surprised to see how well they lived and hoped that, after the war, when they rebuilt London's East End, England would do as well. The natives here were certainly better housed than the majority of English workers. We were impressed with the planning of the town, with the wide boulevards, nearly all of which were lined with orange trees heavy with ripening fruit.

It soon became obvious that the locals had no idea we were going to stay for so long as our welcome seemed to cool off after a week or so and we were left to wander around the town alone.

The shops were full of everything, no rationing, no black out and everyone was well dressed and looking very healthy and prosperous. The locals made no secret of the fact that they were recruiting immigrants for after the war, and there was much offering of job opportunities and exchanges of addresses, with promises to write. However, with the hole in the side of the ship patched up with cement, and a list that was still apparent, we embarked for a destination that, at that time, was unknown.

SEVEN

BEFORE WE SIGHTED land we became aware of a peculiar smell and the sea turned brown. Bombay, the gateway to India, finally became discernible in the haze with its bleached white buildings. There is no other country in the world to compare with the panoramic beauty and scenic grandeur but this pleasure was immediately dispelled by thousands of flies, intense heat, and nauseous smells. Everything, including the dhotis and turbans worn by the thousands of coolies who swarmed on the dockside, were pure white, in the brilliant sunshine, in contrast, our ill fitting drill shorts and shirts that were stained dark brown by our sweat. Issued with only one pair of shorts and one shirt each at Hitchin and worn on the boat, our attempts to launder in seawater with saltwater soap had left noticeable discoloration marks. We were warned to look after our possessions as thousands of coolies confronted us, shouting and jostling, demanding baksheesh, as we made our way to transport on the dockside.

The transit camp was at least a hundred years old, dark and smelly. The old beds were bug infested and there were no mosquito nets. Sergeants had better billets and a decent mess, whilst the officers had vanished. The British still retained the old Victorian attitude of class distinction and class-consciousness. Snobbery still persisted and pretentious standards were taken to extremes. We were not surprised to see a notice stating,

'Officers and their wives', 'N.C.O.s and their ladies' and 'other ranks and their women'.

We were given a meal of soya sausages, beans and mashed potatoes and tea, and there was a walk from the cookhouse to the dining room across a quadrangle. On the way over my sausages suddenly disappeared, then the beans, then most of the mashed potatoes, I was dumbfounded by the speed in which this happened, Johnny had the same experience. We had to congratulate the kite hawks on their speed and accuracy and it was just as well they had taken our meal, as we didn't fancy any of it, anyway. The army name for these birds was shitehawks. They were an asset, as they helped keep India clean. They have been known to swoop and pick up a whole dinner, and leave the plate clean.

Johnny and I decided to go for a walk to find somewhere to eat.

After much walking we found an English sailors club where we were able to enjoy English style eggs and chips with a glass of beer. We spent several hours here in congenial surroundings. It was after two o'clock in the morning when we left the club to get a taxi back to camp. The town was very busy, even at that time of night, with all the shops open for business, the traffic heavy and people crowded the footpaths. Hundreds of coolies were sleeping on the pavements which impeded our progress and everywhere was spotted with red spittle from the chewing of beetle nut, refuse was everywhere, cow and horse dung, and there was a strong aroma of onions and sandalwood. What a filthy place.

We waited at a junction of five main streets where they met to form a circus, and watched as a couple of holy cows got mixed up with the traffic. We had seen a number of holy cows that looked half starved and most unhealthy. We had been warned to keep away from them. As we waited, we first heard then saw a procession proceeded by a native band, so we decided to wait and see what it was all about. As it came slowly towards us we recognized it as a funeral procession with a large band, professional mourners and a bier supported by bearers, with a naked body on top. This band had competition from another band, leading another procession coming towards us from one of the other streets. There were several hundred in this group all carrying banners and flags. We had no idea what it was all about. When the processions met at the crossroads, the two bands vied with each other and a scuffle quickly became a riot when the body fell to the road. Then another group, carrying banners and sticks and other implements, joined the melee, this appeared to be a signal for the whole population to join in. There was now a traffic jam and the cows we had been watching decided to wander over to us, so we moved to a safer location, keeping our hands in our pockets, on our money. The location was not particularly well lit but as we watched, dozens of bundles of rags suddenly came to life and joined in the fighting.

The natives pestered us for the usual baksheesh. As hundreds of ragged and half starved Hindus began to converge on us, we decided to get away as fast as possible. As we went, we heard the sound of windows being shattered and there was much noise and shouting. There were no police. After walking for some time we managed to find a bicycle taxi that got us back to camp in the early hours. Everyone was confined to camp next day and it was later revealed that a full-scale riot was in progress, causing many casualties. There was looting and the wooden roadblocks were torn up and used as missiles to break shop windows. The Indian police were very slow or even reluctant to deal with the disturbance, and it took several days to restore order. When, three months later, we received copies of English newspapers, the riots had been reported as 'anti-British' and obviously intended to influence the British public in favor of Indian independence. We had witnessed what had happened and how the riot had started so we had difficulty trusting any newspaper reports in the future.

Meantime, most of the teeming illiterate millions who scratched around for scraps of food, had never heard of Hitler. India never went to war, even though troops were enlisted into the forces in large numbers. That night was our introduction to India.

We were pleased to entrain for Quetta. The wide gauge railway enabled the seating arrangements in the military coaches to convert to beds, and still have ample room for corridors. These coaches were military, third class. Most Indians traveled fourth class with all their families and cattle and crowded the carriages to overflowing and even managed to travel on the roof.

On the other hand, officers traveled first or second-class, according to rank. Many first and second-class carriages were air conditioned and had separate compartments for batmen or bearers. Our carriage held sixty men and there was a corridor connecting with the cookhouse coach that provided meals whilst the train was in motion. It is not uncommon to spend several days on a train in this vast country. We arrived at Quetta in November 1941. The train pulled into the station in the early morning, and it was bright and sunny, the air clear and exhilarating with the promise of heat later.

Quetta is situated on a plateau, 5,500 feet above sea level, astride the route from India into Afghanistan, with a motor road through the mountains into Russia.

As the train slowly climbed up the Bolan Pass, the air became cooler and bracing, and we entered another world. This pleasant hill station, with a temperate climate, and sunshine for at least ten months of the year, was a favorite rendezvous for all army ranks. Since the disastrous earthquake of May 1935, when more than 20,000 were buried in the ruins, including several hundred British troops, it had become a desert town. Once a garden city, famous for it's orchards and fine rose gardens, it was now parched and vegetation almost non-existent. The huge Hanna Lake that once irrigated the town, disappeared during the earthquake, and the large irrigation channels were now full of rubbish. The cantonment included the famous Quetta Military College that was considered to rival Sandhurst, and where officers were now being churned out for the Indian Army. Other military establishments catered for the training and accommodating of British, Indian and Gurkha troops, many with their families, in married quarters.

We were met on the railway siding by a smartly turned out reception committee which contrasted with our bedraggled appearance. We were reminded that we were in an earthquake area when we came to attention and the ground shook under us and earthquake tremors rolled through the district. Our 1914 pattern pith helmets had become damaged almost beyond recognition during the journey and many were not wearable. Our shorts must have been designed for much earlier times; they had extra large turnups that folded up to the crotch, buttoned there and at the sides. When let down, the cord round the then bottom was tied at the ankles, on top of which puttees were wound, when we had them. We had found it very convenient to carry things in the turnups, consequently all the shorts appeared baggy. We must have looked a comical lot as tall men had short shorts and small men large ones. Some of the men had exchanged shorts to make themselves appear even more ridiculous.

Transport took us to a compound that would eventually become our permanent unit lines. Our hosts, a regular Army Medium Artillery battery, provided us with accommodation under canvas, on the site of our new barracks that was under construction. They fed us and looked after our welfare. Most of the men of the host battery had been in India for some years and we were to join them, until further notice. The effects of war had not yet reached India. In the tradition of the British Army in India, we worked only during the mornings, siesta commenced at the midday meal break until about three or three thirty then, perhaps, another short period for work or parade, then a bath and dress for dinner. We had a short period of acclimatization, parades and inspections as we were issued with new clothing. We soon learned the meaning of the term 'in bed or out of barracks' after being caught for fatigues when abroad during the siesta period.

Our new permanent barracks quickly took shape as several hundred Indian laborers, mostly female, busied themselves on the site. Each basha was made earthquake proof by a unique method of construction. Frames of bamboo poles, tied at the apex of the roof and reaching the ground in an A shape, supported walls consisting of platted cane and straw matting on which a mixture of mud, cow dung and water had been worked by hand by the women. Within a few days of our arrival we began to move into the newly completed barrack rooms. We had new charpoys and overhead wires to support mosquito nets.

Then we were invaded by N.C.O.s from the host battery who seemed to be after promotions. We did not take too kindly to the new discipline. On that first day in our new room, I was just about to enjoy a rest on my charpoy during the siesta, when a sergeant detailed me to report to the battery office.

Our senior officer was a chap who was at Hitchin with us and had recently been promoted to captain. He was acting battery adjutant and I had dealings with him when I worked in the office at Hitchin. It occurred to me that he was going to ask me to become his battery clerk again and this I would refuse. I would rather remain with the guns, at this stage. He invited me into the office, asked me to sit and offered me a cigarette. He talked about promotions and said we would soon become a combat unit. We were the nucleus with the other battery, of a regiment, and a new Regimental Headquarters (R.H.Q.) was being formed. When, at last he came to the point, he asked me if I would like to act as the battery quartermaster, he couldn't promise anything, it would depend on whether the authorities transferred a quartermaster from another unit, but he wanted me to start immediately and learn the job as soon as possible. He asked me if I had ever thought of applying for a commission, but I couldn't afford that and, while he spoke, I thought of all the advantages of no more parades, promotion and more pay. I didn't think it would mean losing the friendship of my colleagues.

My name appeared in daily orders that evening confirming the appointment to lance bombardier. We had always considered a one striper to be the lowest form of army life but this was different, and I wrote home with this exciting news that same evening. So, next morning, as detailed, I made my way to the office of the quartermaster of our host battery.

B.Q.M.S. Holt was expecting me. He knew all about our C.O.'s plans for me. "Come, sit down" he said. "So you're the lucky sod." After introductions he confided that a number of his men had been after the job and there was some degree of resentment, but he wished me luck and said I would need it. We lit cigarettes and he told me something of the history of his battery.

They were a regular army unit; part of a regiment disbanded and one battery had gone to the Middle East to form a new regiment whilst they remained. As they were all regular soldiers and promotion was slow in peacetime, they hoped that all promotions within the new regiment would come from their battery. They had not long arrived from Rawalpindi and had seen service on the North West frontier. He was a regular, had done twenty years service and, as his wife was now in Quetta, was prepared to stay for the duration, he wasn't too keen on going back to Europe as he couldn't stand the climate.

"Well, it's going to take time to get to know all there is to know and I speak from experience. I've been quartermaster now for seven years and I'm still discovering something new. So, what I suggest we do is take it slowly, one step at a time. First you should take over the ration side and feed your battery, I understand your own cookhouse will be ready in a couple of days and this will be as good a time as any to start, So, first, let's equip the cookhouse. I've got some literature and regulations on this I looked out yesterday, wait a minute, ah, here we are," and he produced a folder and several official forms, the use of which he explained to me. He continued, "Now, taking things one-step at a time, you need the correct authority for everything you indent for and your requests must be on the correct forms. You'll need Indian Army orders and regulations and all the amendments, station orders, requisitions, accounting ledgers, ration forms, diet sheets, equipment folios, pay accounting books and you'll want to know where to go and who to see in all sorts of circumstances, so, back to the cookhouse. I'll give you the forms and the authorities and help you make out the indents, and, having got the cookhouse working, we'll go on from there".

I had to learn all the army terms, how to draw 'free' rations, how to account for the nine annas per day per man ration allowance which was spent with the contractor, and dealings with the bank impressed account. He gave me a set of chevrons and got his Darzi to sew them on my shirt, whilst we wrote out indents for equipment.

"You get these forms signed, then you had better see your sergeant major and find out who will take delivery of all the cookhouse equipment, who the cooks will be, then come back here and I will take you round to all the various stores and supply points. We can start then, to accumulate the necessary forms and accounting books. It would be a good idea if we got some desks for you and your staff and I'll lend you a couple of E.P.I.P. tents (English Pattern Indian Police) until your new offices are ready. Oh, and another important thing, don't forget to get a signature for everything you give out." And that's how the job started.

That afternoon I sat behind the steering wheel of a three-ton lorry. I had never driven before and didn't know the first thing about driving, so I had to learn the hard way. 'Q' Holt sat me in the driver's seat, told me what to do, and off we went to Ordnance. I told my comrades about my promotion that evening, and assured them it wouldn't make any difference off parade, but I knew it would. From then on I worked like a demon. Four men were assigned to me to help organize the supply and equipment of the battery, one of whom was Johnny.

Our barracks were soon finished and we moved into a new office building destined to become the quartermaster's stores. In peacetime, Quetta was a garrison town and full of troops but there weren't many left now, and the Ordnance staff was falling over themselves to complete our indents. We had arrived a month later than scheduled so we had a mountain of equipment and vehicles waiting for our indents and collection.

The first vehicles we took delivery of were five three-ton Chevys. One of these was used constantly to train new drivers and it was driven on a set course for so long that it wore ruts in the ground sufficiently deep to enable it to go around on it's own.

The Regimental contractor stocked and managed a canteen for the men. He installed a billiard table and table tennis equipment to attract custom; he had a monopoly of supply and was officially appointed. He kept the cookhouse supplied with fresh fruit, fish and poultry, eggs, etc., in accordance with the diet sheets and money available, and everything had to be accounted for. India was at peace, and our unit was on a peacetime basis. There was no blackout or rationing and as we wasted our time and the country's money, we thought of the folks back home in the blackout trying to cope with the bombing and rationing in contrast to the feverish activity of myself and staff. Those in control had little to amuse them, so they planned an exercise that entailed bringing forward the collection of equipment. Twenty-two vehicles supplemented our transport and eight six-inch howitzers 1914 models, but there was no ammunition.

It was just as well the trip to lower pastures was planned as it suddenly clouded over and became very cold. The surrounding hills and mountains were snow covered overnight and this was the commencement of the Chota monsoon season. Sometimes, the Chota monsoon period at Christmas time was a non-event but the appearance, in the compound of hoards of wild dogs and hyenas during the night and the continuous howling, night and day, signified a change in the weather pattern.

EIGHT

I WAS DETAILED TO the advance party for the trip to Sibi in the Sind desert. The road through the Bolan Pass is only 90 miles. It rises to nearly eight thousand feet and drops, in easy stages, to near sea level. It was not an easy journey. I had to arrange for the tentage and extra rations and the Christmas festivities were brought forward a few days. The urgency in which orders were received put pressure on my staff. Meanwhile news of my second stripe was posted on orders and I became a full bombardier.

We equipped all drivers with poshteens (which were fur coats, all very old and stinking of moth balls), leather waistcoats and every man in the battery had an issue of snow goggles and face masks. We all thought this unnecessary but events proved otherwise. It was early morning, two days before Christmas when the advance party started out. It had been snow-ing all night and the road was treacherous, even with chains, a snowstorm raged as we proceeded up the pass and we were very fortunate that we completed the journey without mishap. The advance party comprised an officer, a sergeant and two-dozen men plus myself. We had eight vehicles loaded with tentage and supplies, plus a number of smaller trucks.

The temperature changed dramatically enabling us to peel off our clothing as we descended to the floor of the desert where it was a pleasant eighty degrees. The journey took eight hours and it was afternoon before we commenced erecting tents, which were distributed over a wide area to simulate war conditions against bombing and they were to be dug in when the main party arrived. There was no sign of life or habitation. We had a late evening meal and a guard was posted but I didn't enjoy the hard desert floor and it became very cold during the night.

Early next morning I was aroused by excited shouting. Seven tents had been stolen during the night, including one in which four men had been sleeping. The incredible thing was that no one heard anything, not even the guards. All the evidence we had was the tent pegs and the ends of the tent ropes.

The main party began to arrive during the afternoon of the next day. They had been delayed by snowstorms and for the next few days most of us had trouble with our eyes, which had become effected by the brightness of the snow, even though we wore sunglasses. Red swollen eyes were a common sight.

Our host battery joined us, and after only one night at the campsite we were on the move further south. Three hundred miles or more and two days later, we camped in the desert at a place near Hyderabad in the Sind. We made a permanent camp that was only about an hour drive from Hyderabad. There were no roads and the terrain was flat. The supplied maps didn't convey much to us. This was an exercise of movement simulating conditions to be expected in Egypt, making use of sun compasses and the new radio transmitter-receivers.

Johnny was an invaluable assistant. The guns were maneuvered over long distances and supply points for the collection of rations changed each day but new map references made little impression on us as we were able to follow wheel track marks and always arrived at the right destination. To ensure a daily supply of fresh meat, a slaughterhouse was established in Hyderabad. A six-foot wall in an old brick building with a stone floor surrounded it. As soon as the animal was slaughtered, dozens of vultures arrived. They perched on the walls waiting for us to leave. I took all the choice cuts and raced back to camp and the cookhouse before the meat became contaminated. The vultures cleaned up the slaughterhouse compound picking the bones clean whilst the sun bleached the remains. If I was early enough, I was able to explore Hyderabad.

One evening, when I arrived back at the camp, I was informed that the O.C. had been looking for me and would I see him. We had been in the desert for three weeks. He was sitting outside his tent when I arrived, enjoying a bottle of beer, so I saluted and said, "Did you want to see me Sir?"

"Ah, yes, how's it going? Any snags?"

"No." I said.

"I thought I would tell you that as from tomorrow your name will be on orders as a sergeant. I've put your name forward for battery quartermaster, so keep your fingers crossed and hope no one of that rank is transferred to us. It may be some days before we get confirmation from records. I'm fed up with waiting for men to be transferred and in any case you seem to have everything going smoothly. I don't expect to get confirmation until we get back to Quetta, I'm sorry, can I offer you a beer? It was a good idea to get the contractor to follow us down here but I had to put a restriction on the sale of beer to two bottles per man and only to be sold after dark, O.K.?"

I had no idea the contractor would follow us and certainly wouldn't have arranged it, and it occurred to me that Q Holt may have had something to do with it.

"Thank you Sir, would there be anything else?" I said.

He then instructed me to ensure that there were emergency rations on every vehicle. He intended to arrange for the men to exist for a day and a night on emergency rations as part of the training. He asked me not to say anything to anyone, as even his own officers knew nothing of his plans and if he couldn't get a message to the wagon lines in time, we would have to dispose of any cooked meals by burying them.

Up until then, I hadn't met up with the contractor. Orders for extra rations arrived for the Christmas extras had been dealt with by one of his staff and I had not seen him. So I went to find him. There were now several hundred tents scattered over the desert as other units had since joined us and they were dispersed over a wide area. The contractor's tents were in the centre of things. He had erected a large marquee where he also had a shop and canteen. I found him at the rear of the shop with Q Holt.

"Hello quartermaster sahib, this is a good camp. Yes? You like beer or perhaps something stronger?" He asked.

"You're being a bit previous aren't you?" I asked.

"You'll be quartermaster soon, you see, when we get back to Quetta you will have nice quarters which I furnish and it will be good, you see."

"By the way, who invited you to follow us down here?" I asked.

"I knew a long time since sahib, when I mentioned to other quartermaster sahib Holt he raised no objections, besides it much too cold in Quetta just now. I go back soon, the day before you go back."

'Q' Holt confirmed it was a recognized procedure for a contractor to follow the unit when on maneuvers, as he could keep up a constant supply of extras, including beer and spirits, so why not take advantage?

I found it most intriguing that the contractor knew what the regiment was going to do, long before the C.O. got to hear of it.

Constant sand storms made life very unpleasant and we were compelled to seek shelter, as it was impossible for the cookhouse to function. We discovered shelter, about half a mile from the camp in a gully, which had a natural ten-foot high cliff of sandstone. The cliff was several hundred yards long and we parked all the vehicles and set up a cookhouse under the protection of this cliff.

The depression in the terrain could not be seen, unless you were near it.

During the night, without warning, a wall of water about four foot high swept over us and carried away most of the cookhouse and much of our kit, even invading the floors of the lorries, soaking stores and clothing. We spent the remainder of that night recovering kit, some of which had drifted half a mile distant. Next morning, it was obvious we had parked in a dried up riverbed. The extraordinary thing was that by midday, everything was as dry as we had first seen it. We never discovered where the water came from or where it went and there had been no reports of any rain in the vicinity, in fact the desert was still dry and sand storms continued.

Shortly after arriving back in Quetta, confirmation came through of my promotion to Battery Quartermaster Sergeant. It was early February 1942 and Quetta was as dried up as it always was, with no sign of the recent snow. In glorious sunshine we worked in shorts and short-sleeved K.D. shirts once more.

Singapore fell on 15th February1942, but that was a long way away from our cantonment and our peacetime army authorities carried on as if the war with Japan was someone else's concern.

Most of the new barrack buildings had now been completed and we settled down as a regular army unit on a peacetime basis. Not knowing how long this false way of life would last; we luxuriated in new charpoys, clean linen and a plentiful supply of food. The contractor supplied me with a boy named Acku who looked after all my needs and taught me Urdu. Acku had seen service in the Army and had been to many parts of the world with Indian regiments. He could speak English fluently. Our clothing allowance provided K.D. bush jackets and slacks and artillery dress uniforms, all made to measure. In addition, special allowances procured a piano, easy chairs for the mess, table tennis tables, dartboards, and all manner of sports equipment. I became secretary to the sergeants' mess that attracted custom from several well-known local civilians and personnel from the R.A.F.

Rangoon fell on 9th March 1942. Apathy still prevailed in Quetta. During April, I received news from home that I was the father of a daughter, born on 18th January, and this made me very homesick. I kept myself busy but was contentious for several days, and did not register the connubial anxieties of others close to me. Relief from my inner frustration came when it was announced that we would once more move off to the Sind desert for exercises, this time with infantry units. The frantic urgency with which the new 5.5-inch howitzers were issued in exchange for the old 6-inch howitzers, made it appear that we would be off to the Middle East very soon. The new guns and the new Bren gun carriers and armored cars were all of Canadian origin and everything was in measured metrics, so that new gun tables had to be compiled. Excitement increased when I was able to collect a good supply of ammunition for the guns and our gunners were told they would now be firing live shells. We had yet to fire a gun. My staff was increased to six and Johnny promoted to full bombardier. An R.H.Q. had been formed and we were going to maneuver as a regiment.

Camp was established in Kalat State, about five hundred miles south of Quetta, in the Sind desert. It was an impressive convoy that motored over the parched desert. Extra vehicles carried a large number of Indian E.P.I.P. tents (about 12ft by 12ft with detachable walls) strung together. These tents made ideal messes for the officers, sergeants and men; we carried six for stores and rations. In addition there were trestle tables and folding chairs, and of course, the contractor followed us.

For two weeks the gunners moved about the desert, digging holes everywhere, whilst infantry advanced under a barrage of live shells and were initiated into the art of desert warfare. Meantime, my staff and I remained at the wagon lines ensuring the hungry men were fed on time. The heat of the desert was unbearable by day and very cold by night, whilst, due to the distance the water truck had to travel, there was always a shortage of water.

The day the exercise was scheduled to finish I was looking out over the desert, counting the seconds between the distant whip-lash of our guns being fired and the ultimate explosion of the shell as it landed, when I saw what appeared to be a convoy approaching camp. Distortions caused by the heat haze made it difficult to distinguish objects at a distance. The flat terrain and no visible division between earth and sky made distance deceptive. It was sometime before we were able to see a large number of donkeys suspended in midair, slowly approaching us. As the convoy came nearer we spotted several dozen men, all in colorful uniforms, astride very small horses, the riders feet almost touching the ground on both sides. They were all armed, that I could see. Following were a group of riders on larger horses, then several camels protesting under heavy loads. They looked a comical sight from a distance. As they neared camp, a number of jeeps, occupied by officers, made off across the desert to meet the expected convoy. This was an official visit from the Khan of Kalat State and the armed men were his bodyguards and servants.

They established their own camp and brought with them gifts of game and rare wines. They were entertained in the officer's mess. Some of the game found it's way into the sergeants' mess but we did not see any of the wine. The party departed early next morning and a few senior officers were entertained by the Khan, at his palace, about half a days drive away. The following day the regiment left for Quetta.

NINE

BACK IN QUETTA I succumbed to my bed as I was running a high temperature. Next morning, as he hadn't seen me in the mess, the R.S.M. visited me and confirmed that a large number of men were suffering from sand fly fever, including the M.O. He recommended bed until the fever left me.

He was always full of schemes to improve the facilities in the sergeants' mess and now he had another and this is really what he had come to see me for. There was a group known as the Bengal Artillery, all Jute Whallas from the mills in Calcutta, who were about to join us. They had purchased their own guns and equipment and had formed a kind of territorial unit at their club in Diamond Harbor south of Calcutta, and now they had all been conscripted. These men, who were of Scottish descent, and nearly all from Dundee, held important posts in the Jute mills as engineers and they would all receive direct commissions, so we would only be a staging camp for them. They would arrive at Quetta over a period of several weeks and the idea was to promote them all to local lance sergeants, unpaid, a few days before their commissions became known to them. It was the custom for everyone newly promoted to 'shout' a round of drinks on entering the mess for the first time, so our mess funds would be expanded considerably. It was fortuitous that as these chaps came and went, the mess became a gambling den that unfortunately distracted us from our contract bridge, as Johnny and Hutch liked a gamble. I was pleased when they had all departed and taken their bagpipes with them. Few refused commissions and remained with the regiment.

It was normal practice for a quartermaster, in those days, to accept gratuities from the contractor and there was always a supply of drinks and cigarettes in my room. It became an ideal spot for a card school and was often crowded and for this reason it seemed sensible to have a lock fitted to the drink cupboard and Acku kept the key. During the recent exercise I met Hutch who had recently joined R.H.Q. as a technical sergeant and he expressed his interest in contract bridge. His knowledge seemed unlimited and he influenced us to expand our vocabulary as he was well educated and spoke with that unmistakable Oxford accent. We discovered that he had held a commission in the Guards but how he lost it remained a mystery. He taught us all he knew about contract bridge.

Next to be promoted to sergeant was both Johnny and Tom. Johnny had been assisting me as rations clerk and I now put him in charge of transport and spares, petrol and oil, and it was understood that, if we ever went on active service, he would be transferred to R.H.Q. These promotions solved the problem of who would be in our card school and Hutch commenced his indoctrination. We often played well into the early hours.

Mail came through regularly, the news from home was devastating, the strict rationing and constant danger of bombing, not only of men but of women and children, seemed so grotesque in this remote bastion of the Empire.

Johnny and I spent evenings walking in the bazaar inhaling the fragrant scent of Geda and Balsa wood. We spent many pleasant hours bargaining and deciding what to send home in the next duty free parcel. I bought lengths of pure silk which had been hand embroidered and had several gifts made. One Darzi made a small dressing gown for each of my children in Lama wool cloth embroidered all over by hand in silk. I purchased two large metal trunks, one of which I retained and began to accumulate things, that I hoped to take home. The other trunk was for sports stores.

Those early days in Quetta were very congenial. In spite of the fall of

Rangoon and Singapore and the situation in Europe, the army here was still on a peacetime basis and taking advantage of being an outpost. The local cinema exhibited new films exclusively for the troops. Here senior N.C.O.s had comfortable arm chairs in the centre of the cinema, officers had settees at the rear and other ranks had to sweat it out on old cinema seats at the front, and, as everyone was allowed to smoke, we were continually being sprayed by an attendant in an attempt to sweeten the air and kill the flying insects. My job kept me busy, the sergeants' mess flourished and we entertained guests in the mess on Sunday evenings. In normal times Quetta could boast of several thousand regular British troops. However the demand for troops in the Middle East had denuded the garrison of it's manpower and now the last remaining battalion, the Lancashire Fusiliers, were suddenly dispatched to Egypt. So we, the only British regiment left, took over Garrison duties and this entailed extra work.

I now became responsible for fifty seven married quarters, which entailed maintenance of the buildings, furnishings, lighting and heating and the supply of rations for the families left behind, most of the men concerned who's families occupied these quarters were on active service overseas. I also had seventy horses to feed. These were stabled near the racecourse.

Before the advent of the internal combustion engine, horses drew the Royal Artillery gun carriages and the same stables were still in use. The horses were an assortment of Polo ponies, hunters, and racehorses, and the ex-professional jockeys, who supervised the stables, were taken on battery strength.

Everything that happened to other ranks was accounted for in part two orders, published daily, which recorded promotions, sickness, postings and enabled army H.Q. to record the movement of every man in the army. Similarly, horses were accounted for in part three orders, each horse having a name, a description and pedigree, on the appropriate forms. Each horse was allocated to an officer. The officers were at the Quetta College and received an allowance to feed and maintain it. The same officer was debited with the cost of maintenance. The officer also received an allowance to purchase riding equipment and saddle and as there was a constant flow of officers, saddles changed hands frequently, in fact, some saddles were often owned by several officers at the same time.

Many additional horses arrived from distant places such as Lahore, Bombay and Karachi and, on race days, were stabled with our horses. Garrison duties entailed the employment of large numbers of men to deliver fodder and bedding for the horses, rations and fuel to the married quarters, and many other duties not directly connected with battery business, so that training came to a standstill. Senior sergeants were put to work supervising fatigues on the married quarters as it became obvious that other ranks could not be trusted. I shared responsibility of running the tote at the racecourse with Johnny. The tote was worked by hand and there was not much for us to do other than organize staff. This was not difficult as it meant free transport to the racecourse and refreshments. We were always able to make our Saturday night entertainment expenses as we got to know the 'good things' from the stables. There were also regular bookmakers on the course. Our C.O., who was master of the hounds and had come out of retirement when the war started, was now very old and feeble.

We were allowed to send home one parcel a month, a practice of the peacetime army. There was no shortage of anything in the bazaar, much of the goods sold were made in Kashmir but we also found many good Indian treasures made in Birmingham, England. Several good eating places were available to us at very reasonable prices and we also provided the military police necessary to supervise that part of the bazaar that was not out of bounds.

Johnny, Hutch and Tom and I were playing bridge late one evening not long after it had been confirmed we would be taking over certain garrison duties. It was past lights out but we decided to complete the rubber. We always cut for partners and in this rubber; Tom and Johnny were partners whilst Hutch was playing the hand leaving me as dummy. I got up from the table and as no one wanted anything more to drink, I called Acku and instructed him to get ready to clear things up, as I wanted to get to bed. We took our game very seriously as we played for four annas a hundred. Hutch completed game and rubber and totaled up the score, we always settled up at the end of each session but no one ever won or lost much.

At the end of each rubber there was a postmortem as we usually maintained silence during play. They had got to know that I had been given the task of taking over the Regimental brothel. There were only six girls there and a madam, all Indians. The military police supervised and were responsible for discipline and their permanent post, which was manned twenty-four hours a day, seven days a week, was next door to the brothel. All the furniture and cleaning equipment had to be checked periodically and signatures obtained, thankfully, my duty finished there. I was due to go with the M.O. on the following Thursday, then once a month, but it wasn't really necessary and, after the first visit, I sent my store men.

The subjects we talked about were insatiable but we never mentioned the word sex, it was usually, bint, cunt or crumpet. It was Hutch who raised the question of the suitability of our battery sergeant major Jenkins as a senior N.C.O. and he wanted to know more about him as he said he may have met him somewhere else, but couldn't place him. I knew something about the man as he had recently spent some time in my office, where he boasted of his sexual exploits. He had completed twenty-one years army service and had been in India for more than eight years at one stretch and hadn't seen his wife or his two children during that time. His wife blamed him for not being able to get home to England and refused to send photographs, so that he now believed he would not be able to recognize his kids if he met them on the street. Every application for repatriation had been refused so he got the idea that, if he made himself a nuisance with some of the top brass, they would do something about him. Hutch had got part of the story from R.H.Q., so, to satisfy their curiosity, I filled them in with the story as told to me by Jenkins.

At that time Quetta was full of top brass, all chiefs and no Indians, as the saying goes, and our Brigadier, who always maintained a discreet distance, had had Jenkins on the mat, as his daughter was 'up the spout' by him. There was nothing the Brigadier could do, other than promote him and transfer him to another unit, and this is what had been happening for some time. He told the Brigadier, he was quite willing to marry his daughter, if he could be sent home to see about a divorce. He boasted that a certain well known top brass threatened to court martial him but nothing came of it and he said that, until they sent him home, he would try to get as many senior officers wives or daughters up the spout as was physically possible. I never doubted his prowess; he was a good-looking man, though weathered. He let me read letters from his victims' fathers and husbands and I don't doubt he meant what he said. However the situation with B.S.M. Jenkins resolved itself some weeks later. The guard had been issued with .410 shotguns with instructions to use them only to help prevent the wild dogs stampeding about the compound during the night. This was beginning to become effective. At about 2 a.m. one morning, the guard took aim and fired into a pack of wild dogs and hyenas who turned about and fled, just as B.S.M. Jenkins was crawling across the compound in an inebriated condition, trying to get back to his bed. He got into the path of the shot. He was taken to hospital, not badly wounded, and that's the last we saw of him. Tom Short was promoted B.S.M. in his place.

One morning, I was alone in the office, contemplating the pile of paper work that had accumulated and nursing a mild headache, when my office door opened and I automatically shouted 'get out'. I found this to be effective. Men were supposed to be on parade and I didn't expect any of my staff back yet. As the door opened wider I could see it was the O.C. and he brushed aside my apologies and sat in a chair opposite. It was very hot outside but he refused the tea I offered him.

"Q." he said, "I thought I would give you advance warning as the Viceroy is going to pay us a visit in a few weeks time and I want everything to look smart. There'll be bags of bullshit, so I want you to see what allowances you can get to buy whitewash and brushes, then every man must have brooms and brushes, the sergeant major will clue you up. I thought you should know from me, as the visit will be very important for the regiment and to me in particular." He was gone before I could make any comment or ask questions, which was typical of him, always to the point.

Garrison duties now involved providing a guard at Government House, where, to the accompaniment of a Gurkha pipe band, guard mounting was a ceremonial affair. In this respect, and to coincide with the Viceroy's visit, it became necessary to clothe the guard in a uniform more in keeping with the occasion and I received instructions to purchase a lightweight Olive Green serge cloth from which battle dress uniforms were made to measure for each man of the guard and, as soon as practicable, the whole regiment was fitted out with the new uniforms. What a waste that was, they looked smart when new but were most unserviceable.

The task of whitewashing the inside of all the barrack rooms had commenced and stones were collected and placed around the entrances to every building and tent and whitewashed, and mosquito net wires burnished.

It was all spit and polish and even the guns and vehicles had special treatment and sparkled in the sunshine. Sergeant major Jenkins was in his element, he had most of the men in the battery on some charge or other but punishments were not harsh. His favorite saying was 'bullshit baffles brains' and who knows, he may have been right.

The great day came when the Viceroy was due to visit. We commenced the parade soon after breakfast. It was almost unheard of that a quartermaster should be on parade and this was the first time for me in many months. At any rate, they gave me a special place on which to stand on the parade ground. Whoever whitewashed the straight lines on the bare earth across the parade ground had done a good job and any desecration ensured the wrath of the sergeant major. Our parade ground, larger than a football field, was sacred. Half a dozen sweepers brushed away all day long and no other person was allowed to walk across it other than the painters and sweepers.

The Viceroy was scheduled to arrive at 1000 hours and stay with us for most of the day. We paraded all that day, were inspected, dismissed, then paraded again with more inspections, several times, and it was questionable whether we would get any meals as all the cooks were on parade. We all began to feel the effects of the heat and had to get out of the sun. However, at precisely 1600 hours his Highness the Viceroy arrived, and left at 1603 hours. Exactly three minutes for all that bullshit. Apparently he got out of his car, walked round R.H.Q., shook hands with various officers, saw the parade lined up on the parade ground from a distance, apologized for being late, got back into his car and drove off.

This was the silly season.

The heat became oppressive as the summer progressed, winds became strong and dust storms and whirlwinds distributed the contents of rubbish bins over the camp area. Hyenas and packs of wild dogs came down from the hills at night to add to the confusion and sometimes a pet dog, of which there were now many in the camp, would run off with the pack.

Late one night the sergeant in charge of the guard broke into my room, pulled down my mosquito net and, kneeling on top of me, on my bed, proceeded to try to choke me. He intended to kill me and in the struggle we rolled off the bed on to the floor. Acku dragged him off and the noise we made brought assistance from the adjoining barrack room, needless to say, he had been drinking. The R.S.M. was soon on the spot and the poor sergeant was eventually stripped down to gunner.

About this time there was the 'Jungle Rudd' episode.

'Jungle' as he was known, was the O.C.'s second in command. He was always unkempt, often drunk and absent without leave. At the outbreak of the war he had already completed seven years service in India and at that time this was considered to be the maximum period of overseas service. He thought he should have been repatriated. He was often missing from camp for long periods and, on several occasions, was rescued from out of bounds areas, usually very intoxicated.

This particular afternoon, he made his way into the O.C.'s office with an Indian girl who was smartly dressed in European clothes and requested that the O.C. marry them. The sergeant major was sent for and he recognized the girl as number six from the regimental brothel, known as Agnes from Lahore. Apparently, the girl had proposed to him whilst he was under the influence and she said she had now saved enough money from her earnings, to get married. Well, the old man did not know what to do in the circumstances, so Jungle was arrested for incorrigibility and they intended to release him next morning. He was the first prisoner to be locked up in the new prison cell that had been built at the end of the guardroom block. The cell window was of regulation reinforced iron bars and looked secure enough. It appeared however, that the mud walls had not dried out and 'Jungle' was able to lift the window out from the wall, frame and all, and escaped during the night. The guard didn't hear a sound as the window was at the back of the building. Some days later he was found in the bazaar a very sick man and was taken to hospital. That was the last we saw of him.

Disquieting news from home that my wife was not well and would need treatment distressed me as I was powerless and didn't know what to do, so I broached the subject with the C.O. He was very concerned and obtained a report from the Army Navy and Airforce Association who had the necessary organization to investigate. Eventually a report came from England that reassured me. They had arranged to send my wife and two children away on vacation to a rest home in North Wales that, I hoped, would solve the problem. Later, the tone of letters seemed to improve but I was not aware, until some years later, what a fiasco the holiday turned out to be. Because of the bombing, my wife always carried all her personal papers with her, i.e., certificates of births and marriage, insurance policies etc. in her suitcase. But the suitcase containing all these things and all the things most valuable to her, including gifts I had sent from India was stolen. Nothing was ever recovered.

TEN

A ROAD RUNS FROM the Caucasus Mountains through Afghanistan and into India via Quetta. The Russians were now fighting the German onslaught in these mountains. So the war, as far as we were concerned, took on a new significance. The two R.A.F. sergeants, attached to our mess who were with R.A.F. Intelligence, made several trips into Persia, near the Russian border and kept us amused with their exploits. They had something to do with Lease Lend but their main concern seemed to be the exchange of whiskey for vodka. Large numbers of R.A.F. personnel began to arrive at about this time and there was an elaborate plan to build an air base. Some weeks later though, there was a scandal when the European contractor went missing with all the funds.

A few hours by road north from Quetta, towards Afghanistan, the plateau rises to about 7,000 feet above sea level, and then plunges down the Khojak pass to the Afghanistan border. Our regiment was deployed along this route to survey and test the defense earthworks being constructed. From the top of the pass, the immense valley could be seen, stretching east and west with, in the distance, snow covered mountains as far as the eye could see. The heat haze made distance deceptive and the hills seemed to float in a sea of mist. We were invaded by groups of tribesmen who, not many years previously, would have been enemies but were now loyal subjects and called themselves King's riflemen, having received the King's shilling. They were peaceful and friendly and demonstrated their homemade rifles, with their long barrels that were deadly accurate. Their main need was for medical supplies and I could never figure out how they managed to live off the land in these barren mountains.

We established an echelon half way up a mountain and the gunners roamed the hills over the border seeking defensive positions. Our surveyors made maps. The giant land turtles were a nuisance in our wagon lines. They burrowed under the lorry wheels and exploded when the lorries moved off, stinking to high heaven. Dung flies, as large as tennis balls and covered in black fur, buzzed around and gathered human waste and odd scraps of food, rolled up small pieces into balls and flew off. I went over the border with the R.S. and we watched a large trading caravan, consisting of several thousand camels, horses and cattle that traveled regularly between Tibet and the Persian Gulf through the Afghanistan valley. The tribe carried everything with them, their women and children, poultry, goats and tents. The caravan took several days to pass any given point and had used the same route for hundreds of years.

On the morning the exercise was due to finish, I was driving back to Quetta when, about ten miles from camp, I was stopped by a Balluchi, the woodchopper who spent most of his time outside our main cookhouse. I could not fail to recognize him as he was six feet six inches tall, was crowned with a huge mop of black hair and a long black beard. He had often been kicked out of our compound when men complained of the noise he made. His prayer time coincided with our siesta period and he performed on his prayer met, kneeling, bowing and kissing the ground and, at the same time, bellowing his prayers at the top of his voice. He told me he was a very holy man and sincerely believed that the louder he prayed the better favored he would be with his god. I stopped the jeep and asked him what he wanted; he explained he wished me to visit his six wives and his many children and his livestock. It became clear to me why he always had several donkeys outside our compound and why he foraged in the cookhouse waste bins for food. He presented me with two live chickens that I accepted but let them go a hundred yards along the road, hoping they would find their way back. Next morning he was outside the cookhouse chopping wood as usual.

That summer the monsoon struck northern and central India with disastrous consequences.

The Indus broke its banks in many places and the river changed course and washed away about eighty miles of the main line railway. We were then cut off from the outside world by rail and road and this, at a time when the Germans were threatening the Russian lines in the Caucasus Mountains. Had the Germans been successful there was very little to stop them from motoring through into India. Railheads were established at each end of the breach in the line and barges were used to transport men and materials between the breaks, until the line could be repaired. The R.A.F. used the few planes available to fly in their personnel from other regions.

Late one Sunday evening the R.S.M. was called to the regimental brothel to assist in quelling a disturbance. Our two men on duty, acting as military police, could not cope and were compelled to call for assistance. In view of the gravity of the situation, those of us in the mess at the time decided to accompany the R.S.M. There were five sergeants, the R.S.M. and myself and we took six extra men. We all carried small arms and ammunition and were in the bazaar within a short time. Apparently, the R.A.F. who numbered several hundred, had been monopolizing the brothel the whole weekend and as the girls had been overworked, the madam had employed an extra girl, unofficially, and this is what had caused all the trouble. She was an Anglo-Indian, very young with fair skin, almost white. The M.O. had not examined her. Several dozen men had forcibly used her, without payment, the fee, incidentally, was only two rupees eight annas, which was about three shillings, When we arrived the R.A.F. men were hostile and we were compelled to forcibly clear everyone from the premises and put the brothel out of bounds. In other words we got to clobber quite a few R.A.F. heads. But this did not compensate for what we discovered.

When the M.O. arrived, the girl was unconscious and had to go to hospital. It was unusual that such a good-looking girl found her way into a brothel. Even though our unit provided a permanent staff to act as military police to supervise the regimental brothel, the hours during which men of our unit were allowed to visit, were restricted. This was designed to avoid conflict with other units and officers. The bestiality of men forcibly separated for long periods from their loved ones is often incalculable and brutal. There were many instances of rape and sodomy but punishments were not severe and the offenders were transferred to other units.

We were prepared to endure the hardship to finish the war quickly and get home. But we were confined to a little known place, playing at peace time soldiering and not knowing for how long it would last or what the future held in store. We lived in a state of unreality and some of the men were unable to cope with this.

The old C.O., who we knew as granddad, retired and a much younger colonel joined the regiment. There was much coming and going of officers and men and with so many men on duty, changes were not noticeable. The bazaar now seemed to be empty of people and we missed a number of civilians who no longer visited the sergeants' mess. It seemed that most of the local population had moved away.

Then I became sick.

For two days nausea attacked me every time I attempted to drink anything. I couldn't eat and found it difficult to concentrate in the office. On the third day the vomiting left me and I was lying on top of my bed with only a towel over my stomach, hoping the violent headache would pass, the store man came looking for me, as Acku hadn't disturbed me. It was not particularly hot outside but I was perspiring freely and my store man acted promptly and, without my knowledge, sent for the M.O. The next thing I knew was that I was in an ambulance on the way to hospital. At the hospital, the first sign was deafness, and then I couldn't stand the light, so the room was blacked out. All I wanted was sleep.

I didn't know I was sedated. During waking moments, I remember people standing over me and on several occasions I recognized the Padre who seemed to be there most of the time. My imagination ran riot as I entered a world of fantasy. By using my arms as wings I found I could fly anywhere, the lift off was so easy. I had the most peculiar dreams, floating across rooftops and looking down on everything, including myself. There was always a feeling of intense loneliness during these dreams. I could float over what I imagined to be the house in which my wife and children were living but it was always night. I could never manage to enter the house or see them. There was always a barrier I could not penetrate.

Early one morning something clicked inside my head and I heard a distant church bell ringing. Then I heard beautiful music playing to the accompaniment of a church organ and choir, the whole being subdued by the sound of running water. This, of course, was ridiculous because there are no churches anywhere near the Quetta hospital. The closing of a nearby door brought me to full consciousness and I could hear and the headache had gone. I wasn't sure where I was, all I knew was that there were various tubes attached to me and I was afraid to move. It was dark when this happened, and I must have slept again. When I woke, the sun was shining into the room with no effect on my eyes.

I still had a sinking feeling and the various tubes attached to me annoyed me. Two male nurses arrived and the M.O. examined me, I resented his prodding and was soon exhausted. The feeling of weakness was beyond explanation, I didn't know it then, but I was lucky to be alive. I had been unconscious for five weeks and had had enteric fever. When I first entered hospital I weighed over thirteen stone and now my weight was down to half that. I felt very miserable and wanted so much to see my wife. I was put on a special diet and within a week started to recover and could have anything I fancied. I drank four bottles of Guinness a day.

It wasn't long before I had visitors. Johnny told me he had written to my wife and told her I could not hold a pen and I was grateful to him. Amongst the mail waiting for me was a photograph of my wife holding my three-month old daughter in one arm and my eighteen-month-old son in the other. They looked so angelic and I wanted to cry. This only renewed my determination that, whatever happened, I would live to see them one day.

One afternoon a male nurse asked if I would see the Indian contractor. He was waiting outside and wanted to see me urgently.

I asked that he be sent in. He brought an elaborate basket of fruit and seemed most anxious that I should get back to duty as quickly as possible. When I asked him why, he said, "I think you ought to get fit quickly sahib if you want to go away with the regiment when they move".

"What's this about moving?" I asked.

"You all go to Bangalore, sahib. Because I get the news first, it cause much trouble".

"Come on then tell me all about it."

"It's true sahib, I have close relative in New Delhi who keeps me posted with all the news that might affect the business and you can take it from me that the Regiment is going to move soon to Bangalore."

He then proceeded to fill in the details as to dates and times and the name of the village we would eventually make camp in and the fact that we would leave Quetta on a certain date on two trains, I found pencil and paper and wrote these details down so as not to forget. If it were true, it made me want to get out of hospital as soon as possible. I didn't want to be posted to another unit and I presumed everyone knew all about it. It annoyed me to think they were keeping this news from me. When the Battery O.C. came to see me that evening, I thought he was trying to get rid of me when he suggested I should take a long convalescence as soon as I was fit to travel, although he was pleased with my progress.

"I'd rather go away with the regiment when we move to Bangalore in about six weeks time." I said.

"Do you feel alright Q?" He asked.

"Yes, why?"

"Look, I don't know where you got that idea Q, but honestly I know nothing about any move and you had better forget it and think about a spot of leave." He said.

Either the contractor was lying or the O.C., so I said. " Look sir, I don't know whether you know anything or not, if you do I don't blame you if you keep the news from me, but I honestly think the regiment is going to move, furthermore, I've got details with dates and times".

"Look Q, we're not moving I can assure you of that, I would have heard by now and I would tell you." He said.

"O.K. if that's how you feel" I said. "But I wonder if you could find out, if I gave you some details?" I handed him the penciled notes I had made when the contractor visited that afternoon.

"How could you get this?"

"From the contractor. He was here this afternoon, said the information came from a relative in New Delhi."

"Good god man, if this is true there's a serious leak of information, so we had both better keep it under our hats. I will try to make some confidential enquiries and if I find out anything, I will let you know, but it might take time."

I had a number of visitors during the next few days. No one said anything about a move.

About a week later, the O.C. came to see me again and confirmed he had been in touch with his friend in New Delhi and couldn't find out anything, so we presumed the contractor's news was a hoax. I now began to think seriously about convalescence and daily bridge games.

I quickly gained strength and weight and was able to walk about the grounds, but it was four weeks before the official confirmation of the move came through. I handed the Instructions and Movement Order from Regiment H.Q. to the O.C. It was marked 'Top Secret'. It was correct in every detail I had previously told him.

The padre was very good to me during my stay in hospital and I am convinced that his prayers and the faith he instilled had a lot to do with my speedy recovery. The M.O. also, was pleased with my progress and when I asked to be discharged he handed me two months medication and a certificate excusing me from all duties for twelve months. The auditors were in my office the morning I arrived back at barracks. I was feeling weak and depressed but my staff was cheered when they saw the certificate the M.O. had given me. They thought this a great joke.

To comply with Indian Army orders an audit was essential. They spent the next seven days looking for surplus stores and checking records. There was a mountain of records and paper work and we had a large amount of surplus stores. This was a court martial offence but the audit staff was easy to bribe. To a Hindu, a bribe was the normal way of doing business and it meant a lot of bartering to persuade the chief auditor to part with a certificate of clearance. It cost a sack of sugar, a case of tinned milk and various other items to gain a little slip of paper that enabled us to have a bonfire of all our records the day after the auditors departed.

As India was not at war, we were liable for Indian income tax on our army pay and we had a battle with the Indian tax authorities. It was the auditors who discovered that, if we paid our liability for tax into the Indian post office savings account for the duration, it could be claimed after the war, and this we did, a separate passbook being issued for every man. As regards pay, we did receive a little extra which was called a rupee allowance but our pay was very much lower than that received by our comrades in arms from other countries. The two New Zealanders attached to the mess were paid nearly twice as much as the pay received by our men of equivalent rank. The ordinary G.I. received as much as our battery captain, furthermore, they expected to be repatriated after only twelve months overseas service.

I was never worried about the surplus stores we had accumulated, this occurred more by accident than design. It started with the first batch of condemned clothing. The system was, that when sufficient clothing had accumulated, considered to be worn beyond repair, a condemnation board was held. The clothing was listed, inspected, and counted and the condemnation certificate, signed by a junior officer, the B.O.W.O.

(British Ordnance Warrant Officer) and myself. This became the authority to indent for replacements after getting a signature from ordnance for the return of the condemned material. On the first occasion, to obtain new stock we forgot to take the condemned clothing but managed to obtain a signature from the Jemadah in charge who wanted some extra food rations. So that next month we had double the amount and so it went on. The system of bartering never got out of hand and we always had plenty of everything. It all seemed a wicked extravagance in view of the dire need in other parts of the world. The waste of men and material during the war will never be accounted for.

How easy it was to indoctrinate a nation to go to war and then create the necessary credit and organize production. The huge fortunes created for those already in command of wealth and the circumstances that compelled a section of the population, mainly youths, to take up arms and do all the dirty work, all under the guise of nationalism, was sickening. I only wish they could do the same thing in time of peace, but we never seem to have the favorable economic circumstances.

I had become accustomed to Quetta and would miss the acquaintance of the many people in the various Army establishments and the companionship and comfort of the sergeants' mess.

Before we leave Quetta let me tell you about the employment offered in ordnance factories and depots. Large numbers of natives gather at first light for jobs and wait in the hope of being selected. They were employed and paid daily. They worked long hours, were poorly paid and had to hand over to the overseer ten percent of their pay as commission, otherwise, no job. Everyone was expected to be dishonest and only the fittest survived. India is a cruel country. Many prisoners brought to work in ordnance factories were chained together all day and some died in harness. Prison sentences were severe and it was not unusual for a man to get ten years hard labor for stealing. There was no probation.

It was no hardship to soldier at Quetta but the prospect of joining up with the forces already fighting was now inevitable. In all the daylight hours of consciousness during the nine months or so in Quetta, I had a constant fear that harm would come to my family back in England and I was powerless to protect them, which was just the thing I was supposed to be doing. It had already been decided when and where we would see action. We were now on our way to Bangalore where the Fourteenth Army was being formed, to eventually oppose the Japanese who were about to advance through Burma.

ELEVEN

THE SANCTIMONIOUS BULLSHIT changed as soon as the regiment was put on a war footing. The paper war came to an end. We feverishly packed and prepared to move. Of the two trains, one carried the sixteen guns and nearly a hundred vehicles, plus sufficient men as a permanent guard, whilst the other carried all the stores and ammunition and the remaining men.

The followers came with us even though they were non-combatants and were not supposed to be on active service. They had all volunteered and only three of them went missing during the journey. Although strictly forbidden, many pets were secreted on to the trains. We had to have an extra wagon to carry the surplus stores.

Attempts had been made to dye our bed linen and mosquito nets that were now various shades of brown. I could see a speedy ending to this luxury as, from now on, we would be doing our own laundry, in fact, within two weeks, these became cleaning rags.

Our train, which carried the main party, moved off first and I was allocated an air-conditioned compartment at one end of a cookhouse coach, of which there were two. Sergeants of the Indian Army Catering Corps occupied the other compartments. The men had military sleeping coaches, whilst the officers had first class carriages at the rear end of the train. We could walk the length of the train, but the officers had to wait for the train to stop to have their meals, as there was no corridor connection.

My compartment contained everything, bunks for four persons, toilet and shower box, and a plentiful supply of water and ice.

As soon as I had deposited my kit, I collapsed on one of the beds. It would still be some time before I became really fit.

The Army Catering Corps would now look after our needs until we arrived in Bangalore in 10 days.

When I awoke, the train was on the move and my colleagues were already in the compartment planning some serious card playing.

We had many stops to pick up fresh rations, water and ice, as well as to change engines. But there was no urgency. The surplus tea, sugar and tinned milk I had distributed, was now enjoyed as, at almost every stop, a procession of men were to be seen hurrying to the engine with their billy cans scrounging hot water for the tea.

For the most part, we of the bridge school ignored the many halts and the passing scenery, concentrating on the game in progress. Nothing was allowed to disturb us until the train arrived in New Delhi. Here we were obliged to join in a route march. I felt I needed the exercise and I went along. The men were dressed in full marching order with bayonets fixed. Although not entitled to, I wore a Sam Brown belt and no one objected, in fact the O.C., was surprised to see me on parade. We marched up the Garstin Bastion Road, then to Patchpuri Mosque and the Red Fort. Here we rested and returned to the railway station via Lower Bela Road and Delhi Gate. It was very hot and humid and I was pleased to get back on the train to change my sweat soaked clothes. This would be the last opportunity to exercise for the next seven days.

One night, we had an opportunity of witnessing one of the Seven Wonders of the World. We were nearing Agra and everyone was on the look out for the Taj Mahal. The train slowed as this splendid mausoleum came into view. We could see this magnificent monument, sparkling white in the brilliant moonlight and, thanks to our army field glasses, were able to enjoy the spectacle. This mausoleum was completed in 1653, before the British conquest of India by Clive in 1757.

It became even hotter as the train traveled south across central India. Most Indian railway carriages were fitted with three sets of windows which could all be let down; a slatted window to shield from the sun, a fly screen and a glass window. But the constant window adjustments made no difference to the air supply. My compartment was fitted with a fan. As we traveled south through Jabalpur, Nagpur and Hyderabad, we spent time observing the constant changing breeds of natives, some extra tall, some short and even jet-black, but most were on the verge of starvation. At one stop hundreds of professional beggars slapped their bare swollen stomachs in unison and begged baksheesh. Then there were the holy monkeys, these huge animals attempted to ransack the train and made off with a lot of the men's kit. In general though, we ignored India as it passed us by and concentrated on the cards. Did we have a premonition that this would be the last opportunity our bridge school would play together? After we had completed the last rubber and totaled up, Hutch was nearly five thousand points in credit, which proved that bridge was a game of skill.

After ten days on the train, it was a relief to find the climate more temperate.

The new campsite was located, surveyed and cleared of snakes and scorpions, tents erected and the trains unloaded. This was not unlike any other exercise.

Our followers soon settled down and actually enjoyed small arms drill. We had a period of intense training in Jungle warfare. P.T. before breakfast was compulsory, plus a round of the newly constructed battle course. At dawn every day, my store man Mac brought me a mug of tea that I drank in bed. I will tell you something about Mac later. Every morning the O.C. came to see me after he had started the men and officers on their P.T. session. He always seemed most concerned about my welfare and it wasn't long before Mac was supplying us both with early morning tea.

This became a habit; I had a makeshift bed in a large tent we used for storage. P. T. was taken seriously and no one was supposed to be excused.

The last obstacle on the battle course was the water jump and so many men jumped into the water that the sergeant instructor from the physical training corps decided that the water should be covered with sump oil. It seemed to me that this would entail a waste of clothing, as many men were not athletic enough to clear the jump, so the O.C. suggested the instructor should complete the course himself to show us how it should be done. Imagine our delight when he fell over backwards into the oil. That finished the water jump.

I was still officially excused all duties, but that didn't prevent me working, although I still felt weak. We were all anxious for action but were apprehensive at the hardships we realized lay ahead. It was now mid-August 1942 and we were with IV Corps. All orders came from IV Corps Command H.Q. Command now came from the top, in contrast to the happy days in Quetta when command came from the bottom.

At Quetta, I was obliged to follow all the rules, regulations and orders that covered everything and accumulated masses of paperwork. Now I had to await orders from the C.O., who duly passed on orders he had received from IV Corps. A map reference signified where rations or equipment were to be collected and Mac and I managed comfortably. During the few weeks at Bangalore things were easy for me. I had, during my wanderings, been able to visit Kola Goldfields and was amazed at the wealth. Here were the deepest mine shafts in the world going down 10,000 feet or more. The town was reminiscent of Welwyn Garden City, but with much wider roads and tree lined avenues. English type houses, churches and cinemas and shopping areas, hundreds of new cars and everyone well dressed. India was full of surprises. For five shillings a box, I purchased boxes of cigars, packed fifty in each box, at a place called Trichonopoly. All the cigars were packed in cellophane and individually housed in aluminum tubes so they traveled well when I sent them home.

Transport was laid on every evening from camp to the centre of

Bangalore, a distance of about twelve miles. We made use of the various entertainment establishments, cinemas and eating-houses and dance halls and there were plenty of shops. At one dance hall, frequented by American G.I.s, a skirmish took place one Saturday evening and developed into a full-scale fight between the Yanks and our men. During the brawl, an American sergeant was thrown out of a window and died of a broken neck. At the court of inquiry, evidence was inconclusive and the hall was put out of bounds. The local police took the matter up and sent the Indian manager to prison for allowing fighting on his premises.

We had been settled in Bangalore for about three weeks when the O.C. at early morning tea, asked if I would like to go on leave, as there were vacancies for three sergeants at Ootacamund, in the Nilgiri mountains. I accepted and asked if Johnny, now with R.H.Q., and Tom, who was now a sergeant major, could go with me. The O.C. was able to arrange this and we left early next morning.

At risk of turning this account into a travelogue, I must tell you of this old fashioned village in the hills, which was a beautiful place. Ootacamund, or Ooty, as it was better known, was a hill retreat in the Blue Mountains, 7,347 feet above sea level and populated by retired army personnel, tea planters, engineers and remnants of an old British aristocracy, transported back to Victorian times. The tiny hill railway climbed up to Ooty in a few hours. The first stop was Goonoor for refreshments. The ratchet safety strips clanked as the little engine puffed away up the one in five inclines and we wondered whether it would ever make it to the top. There were a few English shops, reminiscent of a bye-gone age and the old St Stephens church, the first church I had seen since coming to India. The hills of Ooty are ideal for riding and hunting.

Deciduous forests stretched as far as the eye could see. The eucalyptus trees disinfected the air and had a bracing effect. We enjoyed the luxury of feather beds, deep armchairs and good food. The day we arrived, a European woman was attacked and killed by a black panther just a hundred yards along the road from our lodgings and this prevented us from

wandering out much at night. However, our company was always congenial and we received a number of invitations to play bridge.

We enjoyed plenty of cool walks round the racecourse and Hobart
Park and spent time in the Botanical gardens and the artificial lake at
Kodaikanal. Our leave came to an end and back with the regiment we
became immersed with preparations for the move into Burma.

The movement order was not expected so soon and took us unawares.
In view of what was said about road conditions we still didn't believe we
would ever get there.

Many other units of the IV Corps were on the move and there did not
seem to be a strict timetable and the journey was going to be pretty rough
and subject to rail and road conditions. Most of the regiment's transport
went by road. To Calcutta from Bangalore via Madras was about 1,600
miles. From Calcutta via the broad gauge railway system to Parbatepur
another 235 miles, then, after changing to the meter gauge railway to
Pandu, now about 400 miles from Calcutta, coolies would push the railway wagons onto barges for the crossing of the Brahmaputra. Then on
to the single-track meter gauge rail to Dimapur, another 200 miles and
to Kohima, another 70 miles by road, followed by another journey by
road to Imphal in Assam, to prepare for the final treacherous journey into
Burma. Changing from road to rail was necessary, as roads did not exist
in certain parts.

With military precision and to a timetable, the move commenced.
Positions of each vehicle and the men involved, were listed with times
and places in the convoy. There was always doubt that the roads would
not stand up to heavy military traffic. There was a bottleneck with the
toy meter gauge railway link, in addition, it was doubtful whether the
jeep tracks into Burma would be adequate to take our heavy guns, so it
was suggested we were wasting our time in attempting the journey. The
day before the main convey left, our small party was transported to the
train that would take us to Calcutta. The guns were loaded onto flat-
topped railway wagons, as were the Bren gun carriers. In addition, several

hundred rounds of 5.5-inch ammunition were loaded. There were sufficient men to handle the load and provide a guard for the journey. Our train moved out on the same day as the road convoy moved off.

Accommodation for the five-day journey was in military coaches with a cookhouse wagon. With our party there were two sergeants, of whom Lofty was one. Mac, my store man, and all the bridge players went with the road convoy.

When the train reached Calcutta, our coach and several goods wagons were detached from the main train and shunted into a siding. I was left with twenty-four men, plus the two sergeants and a second lieutenant. We were detailed to get the ammunition, and ourselves, up to Diaper by the river route.

Several days later, our part of the train was moved and shunted on to a siding at a place called Dhubri. Here was a four hundred yards long pathway down to the river Brahmaputra and a landing stage. The river was wide and to get across it required traveling upriver against the fast moving current to the landing at Pandu, a distance by water, of about 140 miles. The journey up river took approximately 36 hours with only about 12 hours for the return trip. The Americans were building the Ledo road into China, about 1,800 miles long, cut through virgin country. The river route was being used to transport hundreds of thousands of coolies for this purpose. They say at least a million coolies were involved in the project. When we approached the landing stage, we were confronted by thousands of coolies waiting for river transport to take them on the first stage of their journey. The Yanks had recruited whole village populations and they carried all their possessions including animals. This was the hottest time of the year and very humid. There was no shelter from the sun, no wind, and the air was filled with the stink of sweating bodies, cooking and human excretion, whilst the buzzing of millions of flies matched the noise of the thousands who continued their dialogue well into the night. No matter how many coolies departed each day, the mass of bodies never diminished.

TWELVE

ONE OF THE longest rivers in the world, the Brahmaputra was a natural obstacle and it took all the resources of the Fourteenth Army to move the massive amounts of men and material across it. The recent monsoon had disrupted traffic but as soon as things got back to normal, there was an earthquake, which threatened to put the toy railway out of action for good. However, hundreds of boats had been requisitioned from all round the coast of India and down to Burma, in a similar manner to the Dunkirk operation.

When we first approached a boat, we were confronted by hundreds of coolies fighting to get aboard, as whole village populations insisted on keeping together. Each boat, and there were a large variety, was considered to be fully loaded when the Plimsoll line, if there was one, couldn't be seen. They each held on average about a thousand people. At first, we found it difficult to find space to load our ammunition. Each shell weighed a hundred pounds, which meant someone had to get off the boat for every shell loaded. It was subject to agreement with the skipper as to how much ammunition he took. We soon found the best method of loading was to wait until the boat was full and the hullabaloo had settled down. Then we would load, say 100 shells, and arrange with the skipper as to how many bodies got off. This was hard work, in fact, more exasperating and much more demanding than carrying the shells in the first place. However, as our only officer went with the first load and decided to stay at the other end of the journey, to supervise labor there, we ran into a snag.

The coolies didn't want to recognize any of us as having any authority over them so we had to dress Lofty Smith up in my Sam Brown belt and revolver, with an officer's cap and stick. He started yelling at them in a mock English officer's accent and we had no further trouble.

I traveled with the second load and returned on the same boat.

The boats were of all shapes and sizes and caution was necessary as some were so old and fragile, but we were able to send at least one load a day.

On my second journey up river, the boat got stuck on a mud flat for 24 hours. Whether this was deliberate I never understood, but during that day all the passengers crowding the decks, celebrated a religious festival of some kind, whilst I ate and slept in the comfortable cabin of the Dutch captain next to the bridge.

Stripped to the waist, we covered our bodies with coconut oil and carried the shells the four hundred yards from the railway wagons to the boats, on our bare shoulders. I think this must have been the hottest time of year in the hottest part of Bengal, as we perspired freely, night and day. We were thankful for the spare bags of salt brought from Quetta. I bartered some to purchase extra comforts for the men. The Australian bush hats issued in Bangalore were the most sensible item issued to us.

I could see thousands of alligators on the riverbanks shoulder to shoulder. As our boat passed they silently slid into the water. With our stock of ammunition diminishing I sent men ahead to stay with the loads. Those remaining traveled with me on the last boat. It took four weeks to move everything.

We now had to wait for railway wagons to Dimapur on the narrow gauge railway but there was no sign of the remainder of the regiment. Our accommodation was in makeshift camps whilst we waited for the train. It was another five weeks before wagons became available. It is only about 70 miles on the toy railway from Dimapur to Kohima. This was the only route possible. There were no roads, the little single line railway line cut through the jungle most of the way and the Fourteenth Army was being moved along this route.

At Kohima, we found another temporary camp and waited for the arrival of the regiment. Near this camp was a pond in which we were able to swim and launder our clothes. We shared it with the local cattle. A party of Americans arrived one day, reinforcements for a force known as Merrill's Marauders. They were huge, jet-black, over six feet tall, and smoked large cigars all day. There were only eighteen of them, each followed by several coolies carrying their 'canteen' and several cases of beer. Each man had twenty-four cases of beer and six 'canteens', one for every month they were expecting to stay in the district. As they would not be allowed to take that lot into the jungle with them we played these fit young black Americans at water polo. The prize for the winners would be the beer and their canteens. How did a bunch of skinny underfed English working class lads beat them? I don't think they figured it out. Next day, they left the camp area empty handed and we believe, relieved. They were good sports but very bad at arithmetic. We not only won their beer but other luxuries such as Hershey bars, the first chocolate we had eaten in years. And we wondered what we would do all the condoms we had won and the nylon stockings. These came in handy keeping our gear dry later, in the jungle.

Remnants of the regiment began to arrive and early one morning, the guns and the last of the vehicles were unloaded and we were able to function as a regiment once more. It was more than four months since we had left Bangalore.

The road is only about 100 miles from Kohima to Imphal but was very treacherous, full of hairpin bends and steep hills. It was just wide enough to take single line traffic, so that we had to proceed with caution, especially the heavy tractors towing the 17-ton guns. The road, a virgin track, cut out of the sides of the hills, was always precipitous on one side. This small distance took us all day. I was in the driving seat of a three ton

Chevy, waiting on the road for the convoy to move off again, when the road suddenly fell away from underneath me, the lorry sank up to it's axles on the near side of the precipice and, as it came to rest, I stepped out on to the road, expecting to see the lorry overturn and plunge down the thousand feet drop. Fortunately, I was immediately behind a heavy workshop truck that made short work of pulling my vehicle out on to the road again. That night the regiment camped by the roadside before entering the Imphal plain.

Another unit had recently occupied the campsite as slit trenches had been dug and the site fortified. We had a late evening meal and a few tents were erected for a command post and guardroom. With a guard posted we had our first stand-to. We would now stand-to for one hour before sunrise and one hour at sunset, every day, from now on. We thought this was a waste of time as, so far as we knew, the nearest Japs were at least a hundred miles away, so we didn't take it too seriously. However, we had settled down to sleep in the slit trenches when the shooting started.

At first, there was just one solitary report of a rifle shot, followed by the scream of a projectile, as it raced through the air. Everyone was alerted and we had to stand-to again. Some minutes later, another report rang out, followed by several more shots, then it settled down, with only an occasional shot, from a greater distance. Just as we had hoped it would be quiet for the remainder of the night, someone fired several rounds from a machine gun, which we identified as a Bren, then the battle seemed to spread. It soon became clear that a large number of small arms were being fired, as all hell was let loose and tracer bullets found their way into our camp position. Red tracers passed overhead at about knee high and bullets ricocheted off rocks and trees all around us. There were several explosions as grenades were thrown but we kept our heads down and held our fire as instructed. This was our first baptism under fire and it was a frightening experience, as we didn't know what to expect next. We were compelled to stand-to all night as the battle raged, and only finished when the sun came up. Next morning we discovered our only casualties was one flat tire and a hole in one of the cook's tents.

Some time after breakfast we found out an Indian guard who challenged a movement on the barbed wire had sparked off the battle. Empty tins tied to the wire began to rattle. As there was no response to his challenge, he fired. A stray water buffalo was caught up on the wire. There were two Indian regiments here, one on each side of the road about a hundred yards or so away from us. They couldn't see each other through the thick undergrowth. What happened was that both sides thought they were being attacked and in the dark, fought their private war. Both sides had casualties and it was estimated that at least a hundred thousand rounds of small arms ammunition was wasted.

We moved soon after breakfast, nearer to Imphal, to be as far away from any other unit as possible.

A day later, our sister battery left us, and motored to the opposite side of the Imphal plain and south to the Tiddim Road.

With R.H.Q., we made camp in an evacuated Chin village. This was a pleasant spot, the bamboo houses, built on poles, were clean and dry and the clearing was large enough to park all our vehicles. Other army units had been here before us and we had no need to dig trenches again. There were many unoccupied Chin villages in the district, in contrast to the villages perched on the summit of the surrounding hills, still occupied by the Kagas. It was suggested we would soon be sent further south and would see action. Our first aid facilities were expanded and we had to get rid of all our insignias. One effect of all this was that the prospect of action and danger brought the men closer.

We were to be under cover in the village when the rain began. We didn't expect too much rain, as this was the Chota monsoon season but soon the surrounding jungle was saturated. It was so heavy it penetrated the flimsy roof of the bashas so that we were constantly wrapped in ground sheets. We were not sure what day it was, every day was the same, but we knew it was December and near to Christmas. It was almost certain we would not move from here whilst it rained, so we erected tar-paulins by winching wires between trees, built tables and forms from local bamboo, of which there was an abundant supply and put the cookhouse and a place to eat our food, under cover. Anything to keep us busy. I was bored and despondent. My daily task of collecting the rations took no more than an hour a day and, for the most part, we sat around smoked and talked. No one seemed inclined to sit down to a game of cards and the few books some possessed were jealously guarded. We hadn't received any mail since we left Bangalore four months ago.

To relieve the monotony, men attended lectures, usually by troop commanders or for that matter, by anyone who had an interesting subject to talk about, but this idea was dropped as the men became disinterested and the repertoire of dirty stories became exhausted.

As the enemy was getting nearer we were ordered to patrol our own area twice a day before stand-to every morning and evening.

Each patrol was made up of ten men under a senior N.C.O., who patrolled an area outside the base compound making a circuit of about half a mile around the base, at a different point each day.

The jungle was so dense that it was possible to get lost a hundred yards from base, and that's what happened to me the first time I took a patrol out. None of the men allocated to me had been on patrol before. The idea was that the patrol had to be spaced out at five-yard intervals and keep in touch by sight. Complete silence was essential. A bombardier was the leader, I was number five in the centre of the patrol, with a lance bom-bardier at the rear. Everything seemed to go according to plan for the first hour; the leader had only a compass and a machete, which he had to use constantly as we went up and down hills and across streams. It was very wet and we didn't realize it at the time, but we were plagued by leaches. They squeezed themselves through the lace holes in our boots. When I estimated we should have been nearing base, I called a halt and we had a conference, as it would be dark soon.

By the time we decided we were lost, after our third conference, it was pitch dark. We forgot all precautions and ended up holding hands trying to retrieve our steps. It was after midnight and teeming with rain, when we finally arrived back at base. We struck the main road about a mile away from base. Although we had been reported missing, no one challenged us. Everyone was sleeping peacefully in our basha and my repertoire of salty jargon was greatly increased. I wasn't anxious to go out on another patrol.

Some days later, the morning patrol reported they had come across a wild boar. We formed a party to hunt this beast for our Christmas meal. I accompanied them and about three hours from base we shot it. It weighed over three hundred pounds and we took turns to carry it on stout bamboo poles. It made an excellent Christmas meal as the cooks roasted it on a spit over an open fire. We consumed it with local wine I had been able to barter for salt. This made a welcome change in our diet, as we were heartily sick of our food. Fresh meat was non-existent; all we had were dehydrated goat meat and corned beef. Even fresh vegetables were in short supply. IV Corps H.Q. issued rations every day for a full regiment. Half the regiment was a hundred miles away. And because IV Corps H.Q. was never wrong, I decided to say nothing. The extra rations of tea, sugar and cigarettes were a godsend during those weeks of frustrated anxiety as we waited to battle with the Japs.

When the rain eventually ceased we took stock of our position.

THIRTEEN

THE IMPHAL PLAIN, 40 miles long from north to south and 20 miles wide in parts, is surrounded by jungle-covered hills. A tarmac road on the eastern side terminated at Palel in the south and our base was about half way along this road. One afternoon, under a clear sky, we attended a concert. The whole thing turned out to be a fiasco. A piano on a lorry provided the accompaniment for a female singer who bellowed out a few war songs and a Lancashire comedian told a few corny jokes, but most laughter came from the derisive banter of the audience. Never mind, the performers earned a Burma Star.

There were now signs we would soon be moving into the battle zone. I exchanged my vehicle for a Willys jeep, with trailer and a number of vehicles were exchanged so that we now had all four-wheeled drive lorries.

For the first time mepacrine tablets were delivered with our rations. These were a preventative against malaria.

We were pleased to be on the move again, it had stopped raining, and became very hot and humid. Our destination was the Tiddim Road area on the opposite side of the Imphal plain and we followed our sister battery. During the previous weeks we had received a number of reinforcements and I was sorry when Lofty Smith and his gun team was transferred to our sister battery to replace casualties. As soon as we arrived at our new rendezvous, we dug in and were exposed to the sun amongst the paddy fields. We dispersed over a wide area and were well camouflaged.

A few days later a large party of Japanese troops had taken refuge in a village some miles south of us and the local inhabitants had escaped. Our gunners were given the task of softening up the target by shelling, before our own infantry entered the village. There were two villages in this area, spaced about half a mile apart. All the villages looked the same, with a few palm trees, huge clumps of bamboo and a bullock track leading up to a few bamboo bashas on poles, surrounded by miles of paddy fields. The plan was, one gun would take position at a pre-reconnoitered place and with no registration, would fire in accordance with a predetermined fire plan, then withdraw immediately. Success would depend on the element of surprise. A last minute alteration to the plan was that the R.A.F. would bomb the village occupied by the Japs, and this would not only help in the softening up process but would also be practice for the bomber crews.

Our O.P. party joined the infantry, the guns moved up and we waited. About half a mile from the target, I drove my jeep along a bund that was a bullock track near to the second village where several vehicles were already parked, preventing any further progress. The track was only wide enough to support the jeep with a drop of four feet to paddy fields on either side. I had a good view of both villages. The occupants of the other vehicles were on the same errand, as observers, to watch from a safe distance. There wasn't room enough to turn round and we would have to proceed into the village to reverse.

The Lysander bombers were twenty minutes late, then, to our consternation, dived on the village nearest us, which held the villagers. They dropped their bombs and, at the same time, our gunners shelled the other village. We, that is, those of us watching from the bund, went to ground as the bombs exploded on the village nearby. We could hear the screams of pain and anguish of the victims, as the bombers flew away. It was a ghastly mistake. The natives were not prepared for a friendly occupation force to bomb them without warning and casualties were severe.

The half dozen occupants of the vehicles parked near me rushed into the village to give what assistance they could and I followed. Several bashas were alight and mutilated bodies were scattered everywhere. The women were away from the village at the time working, and the casualties were mostly children and elderly men. There had been no chance of escape from their pole huts, as anti-personnel bombs had been used and the unsuspecting villagers were either in their huts or the children were playing nearby. We dragged away those we could see near the burning buildings. But the screams of the wounded and moans of those near death was overpowering. There wasn't much we could do for the wounded as we were not prepared. Pieces of flesh and mangled bodies were entangled in nearby foliage and when I picked up a child's severed limb, nausea and disgust overcame me. All the villagers, dead and wounded were evacuated. To make this bloody mistake even worse, no Japs were found in the other village. Another example of war by remote control. There were many debates about this incident but no one was willing to take responsibility for this ghastly balls up. The authorities agreed it would be best to forget the whole thing as quickly as possible. This incident was very disruptive and caused anxiety amongst us, so we were kept on the move for the next few days to help counteract the effects.

Early in April we were warned the enemy was close by and we dug in off the Tiddim Road. There had been a lot of air activity and the rumor was that the Japs had infiltrated behind us. We hadn't heard or seen anything unusual, until one night at about nine o'clock we were attracted by the sound of singing and shouting coming from the direction of the hills six hundred yards away. A stand-to was ordered and it was not long before we saw hundreds of fairy lights moving down the hill towards us. We had previously been warned that the Japs had done this sort of thing before. The object was to get us to expose our position and even put us to flight, as had happened to certain Indian units.

Four of our guns were in position to fire over open sights and they were brought into action. The effect was dramatic. All the lights were instantly extinguished. We stood-to for the remainder of the night. We didn't hear another sound. Next morning after breakfast, we saw six little

Japs in full war cry, running down the hill as fast as they could, across the paddy fields. As they charged, we mounted two Bren guns to cover their approach and waited until they reached our wire. Just before they reached the wire they commenced firing their automatic weapons, spraying our position. Our Bren gunners silenced them. The whole incident was pitiful. These little chaps were so young; they looked as if they were just out of school. They couldn't resist harakiri. What a waste. Later that day patrols found a large number of bamboo poles with cross poles attached on which they had fixed the fairy lights. Further evidence of the accuracy and devastation of our gunfire. The patrol party found a number of bodies, but no further attacks were made.

We continued to receive movement orders and occupied several different positions and, as the enemy infiltrated, an O.P. party consisting of a troop commander and two signalers was sent out. They joined an infantry battalion in defense positions that our guns were to support.

One morning a few days later, the troop commander, after several days at the O.P., made an unscheduled appearance at our gun position, on his own. He had deserted his two signalers and taken the jeep, their only means of transport. The O.P. was situated in very rough country and even after leaving the jeep track, there was still a good days march both ways. This troop commander was in shock when he arrived at the gun site. He had lost his nerve during an enemy attack and panicked. He remained secluded in his dug out and no one knew what was really wrong or what had happened to his two signalers. He had been a boastful man and was not expected to be a coward. Some days later we learned the infantry position had been overrun by the enemy and retaken again. Meanwhile the two signalers walked most of the way back to the O.P. carrying all their equipment including the portable radio, which they used on the way. I was not at the gun site at the time, so I didn't know what happened to the officer.

Later, when Tom caught up with me I asked him about the two

signalers who met their troop commander the day they returned from the O.P.

"Matter of fact Q, I was on my own in the command post at the time the radio call came through, the duty signaler had just gone out for a piss. These two signalers (he mentioned their names) sounded very cheesed off and told me where they thought they were, so I arranged for a jeep to collect them. They hadn't had any food for three days and emphasized they wanted to see their troop commander, on their own, and, being alone with him they hoped to ascertain why he had deserted them. At the time this sounded as if they were sorry for him, so I agreed. I also agreed to say nothing about it to anyone. Well, fuck me, I didn't expect anything dramatic to happen."

I let him consider what to say next and we both lit cigarettes and inhaled deeply. Tom, who was distressed, continued.

"I don't know if anyone will ever know the true story Q, apparently, the poor sods had a rough time up at the O.P., and to be left on their own in the middle of a battle, compelled to carry all that kit for three days, with nothing to eat or drink, was no picnic. I didn't tell anyone they were on their way, only the driver of the jeep knew anything about it and I swore him to secrecy. The two signalers went straight down into the troop commanders' dugout and surprised him and some angry words were heard outside. Apparently, when threats were exchanged, the troop commander drew his revolver and threatened to shoot it out. After that, the whole incident became confused. When I was near the dug out I heard two shots and warned those who wanted to go down into the dugout to keep clear. I went in immediately to see what had happened and the troop commander was already dead. Two shots were made from his own revolver. That was certain. I've asked myself many times whether I was right in being both judge and jury and if I should have gone further into the matter and had an enquiry. Looking back, this bloke was a bit of a shit to leave his men in the lurch and, as you know, he was never on very good terms with anyone. I still find it hard to believe he could have shoot himself twice but, as everyone's sympathy was with the signalers, I made an on the spot decision that it was an accident. And I'm not going to budge from that. I know this Q, we can't tolerate cowardice and I'm not condemning anyone for what happened. I think I would have done the same thing in their position and if anyone disagrees with me, I'm willing to jack in my fucking rank at any time they like. I hope it will be a lesson to others. You know Q, we're all going to go through some pretty rough times before this fucking lots over. By the way, I really came to tell you we're moving before first light tomorrow morning. Better start loading the four hundred to get ready to move off. They've found a spot on the other aide of the plain, near Palel and we may be staying there until after the monsoon. We can have a hot meal when we've settled in."

FOURTEEN

THE PROLONGED BATTLE of Burma has been well documented and the ultimate success of the campaign is attributed to the bravery and courage of the men of the Fourteenth Army and Wingate's Chindits. But the most significant cause of the Japanese failure to succeed in their objective was the effect of the monsoon of 1944 on their extended lines of communication. We had no idea what was in store for us when we entered the deserted village or that we would be saturated in two monsoons before we were relieved. It was June 1943 and there was a year of uncertainty and suffering ahead.

There were several bashas, all built on poles, in the deserted village and we occupied the best of them including one long communal basha. We used all the old tentage and tarpaulins we could find to try to make the roof waterproof. We made ladders to give us access. In the event of enemy attack, which seemed highly unlikely, we built several fortified posts of earth filled sandbags strengthened with stout bamboo, high enough to shelter in and at the same time escape the expected floods. It was considered useless to dig trenches. Having completed this work boredom and frustration descended upon us, as we perspired in the high humidity and suffered the millions of flies.

A welcome break came when we attended a performance by the Royal Assam Dancers. The concert was organized by IV Corps H. Q. Engineers had constructed a large stage set in a natural amphitheater near Imphal.

Several hundred troops attended. The dance group had the reputation of being comparable with the professionals of Europe. It was a delight to watch the large troop of young girls attired in beautiful native costumes supported by a native orchestra with their Indian music. The precision and discipline of the troop was remarkable especially with so large a company and, as each dance was explained over the P.A. equipment before it commenced, we were able to understand what they portrayed.

What amazed me was the manner in which the men showed their appreciation. It was like being at a Prom concert. Next day I discovered the cause of their good spirits. Each gun crew had been equipped with two shoulder packs containing two half-gallon vacuum flasks. These were supposed to be for use when hot meals couldn't be delivered by any other method. Meantime, the gun crews had purchased local rice wine in the villages and stored it in these flasks. This brew, known as 'Zu' was inexpensive and very potent. This explained their enthusiasm and applause.

The monsoon broke in the middle of the night. Thunder boomed and crashed in staccato detonations. The concentration of thunder and lightning flashes with the illuminated forest, left us all in wonderment at this extraordinary natural phenomena. And it kept us awake. The annual local rainfall was between two and three hundred inches, but it all fell upon us in a very short space of time. The rain bucketed down from the stricken clouds in great sheaves of foaming water; it cascaded and roared finding its way to earth. Our roofs leaked, our clothing and bedding became saturated and before morning, we were all wet and miserable. The war came to a standstill, we were in the middle of a great lake and still the rain poured down.

It was many days before we were able to distinguish where the road was, so we had to use Tommy cookers and we lived out of tins, whilst the flooded paddy fields became our latrine. Leeches were a serious problem. However, as soon as the storm, which seemed never-ending, had lost its first fury, I was able to get the jeep out onto the road and I was mobile again. One day I watched a group of local natives dragging their nets across a flooded paddy field catching fish. This is one of nature's miracles as the ground had been dry for several months. The same fields were fished every year before the rice sowing, and it was amazing the size and number of fish they caught.

At first the natives were reluctant to sell their catch as they dried and stored the fish but I bartered some in exchange for bait and we had them for breakfast.

Despite the rain, and the fact that many roads were impassable, remnants of the 17th Indian Division, evacuated all the way from Rangoon, were now passing our base, on their way back to India and we helped them where ever possible. The poor sods were in a sorry state, having marched several hundred miles through some of the most inhospitable country in the world. Meantime reinforcements, all on foot, were being sent forward and I couldn't help feeling pity for them in their wretchedness. The poor devils were covered in mud, saturated, tired and hungry, and the mules they led were in the same state. 1 am certain we would have been sent forward if the jeep track over the hills had been in a fit state to take our heavy lorries and guns. However, the enemy was having the same difficulty and everything was quiet.

Hutch and Johnny were able to spend a great deal of time in our basha and with Tom we managed a few games of cards, sometimes joined by Taffy Jones and Bill Lowe but there was no gambling as we hadn't had any pay since leaving Bangalore.

Bill was the last of the Jute Wallahs from Calcutta to join us in Quetta. He wouldn't accept a commission and was promoted to sergeant. A heavy drinker, he never seemed short of whiskey and where he obtained it was a mystery. He asked to play cards with us one day, as he was bored, and, half way through the game, threw his hand of cards across the room with the comment: "Aak shit", then, from under his bedding roll produced a number of bottles of spirits. He insisted we celebrate his birthday, and it wasn't long before he began to lead us in a song and dance. When he was in his cups everyone was his friend, he loved to be the life and soul of the party. He was giving us his impression of a highland fling, when he accidentally knocked our only hurricane lamp off its hook. Paraffin spilt over our bedding and when it ignited, we had to work fast to save the basha.

Bill consumed a great deal of whiskey that evening and we had to put him to bed. During the night, he awoke and fell over us and started to urinate in all directions, as we lay beneath him. When we tried to restrain him he said:

"Jesus Christ, the bloody train's not in the station", then, " piss off, we must put the sodding fire out somehow." He couldn't remember anything about this incident next morning.

As it continued raining, we were compelled to spend most of our time in the basha, lying on the floor on our blankets either sleeping, writing or talking. That day I had collected an issue of postage free airmail letter forms which, until our hurricane light became too feeble to see by, kept us busy. Several bags or mail arrived with the rations so we had no cause to complain in that direction, but we had plenty of other grievances. The cigarette ration was one. The free issue was fifty cigarettes per man per week and, normally, they were Wild Woodbines, which weren't too bad, but there had been a holdup somewhere in supplies and the issue was now Victory V. These were putrid, wouldn't burn and were always damp. Someone must have made a fortune out of them. I had so many complaints from men and officers that I had to make several special journeys into Imphal to try to exchange them but it was no use. The cigarettes were packed packets of ten, in airtight tins and we often found they had started to decay and were swollen with dampness when we opened the tin. We could only surmise the tobacco, if it was tobacco, was damp when the cigarettes were packed.

I mention this as Victory V cigarettes could have caused a revolt amongst the troops in this area. Here we were, cut off from the outside world, wallowing in mud and shit, plagued by mosquitoes and leeches, hungry for fresh meat, bread and vegetables and compelled to suffer this indignity because someone in the Indian supply authority had decided that Victory V cigarettes were good enough for us. Many men were suffering from dysentery, some had jungle sores, which couldn't be cured, but most were depressed and morale was at a low ebb. It was the consensus of opinion that these cigarettes were an insult to the British army and IV Corps H.Q. must have got the message as Victory V's suddenly disappeared from the ration and we had supplies of Woodbines, pipe tobacco and, for the non smokers, chocolate, for the next few weeks. I hope you won't think I'm quibbling over this, as there were plenty of other problems; boots were starting to fall apart, none of us had any decent underclothes or towels. Any kit being replaced was impossible.

As it continued to rain our engineers improved our pressure cookers with the addition of empty gas cylinders and hand pumps. The system, when it functioned, burned heavy engine oil with a water drip feed, and produced a flame 20 feet long.

Most of our men now had dysentery to some degree and a large number had weeping sores on their legs.

Maybe it was because of my earlier bout of enteric fever and the medication I took but I seemed to be insulated and was reasonably well. One thing did worry me were my peculiar dreams. The more I tried to resist, the more I seemed to dream. It was always the same. I had only to lift my arms, take a deep breath and push off to fly over the jungle, over the tree tops and often, over the roofs at home, looking down, always looking down, even on myself. These dreams often repeated themselves and although we discussed dreams, amongst other things in the basha at night, I never revealed my own dreams lest I was held to ridicule. The remarkable thing was that these dreams didn't start again until we commenced taking vitamin tablets to supplement our diet.

One evening Hutch came up to our basha with what he held out to be a new pack of cards. It had been sunny all day, the first, fine day for nearly six weeks and we were all feeling the benefit of the warmth. Everyone had been busy bathing and washing and apparently Hutch had washed the cards and dried them in the sun, then used talcum powder on them. He promised to do the other packs in due course. We were sitting in a circle, in our basha on the floor around a blanket spread out and our only hurricane lamp hung from the centre. The conversation went something like this.

Hutch: "I'd give anything for a new pack of cards. Pity you can't get some in Imphal, Q. Perhaps Bill could get some from the same source he gets the whiskey?"

Tom: "This is the old pack, did you clean them?"

Hutch: "I couldn't send them to the cleaners now could I?"

Taffy: "It's all you blokes think about. Why not talk about crumpet for a change?"

Bill: "Or food"?

Johnny: "There's s little cafe near my mother-in-laws shop …"

George: " Where you can get so called fish and chips …"

Johnny: "I suppose your Liverpool fish and chips are better?"

George: "Of cause they fooking are."

Taffy: "I bet if we had a woman each now, you wouldn't know what to do with it, George."

George: "Fook off! I'll be getting some when my transfer comes through."

Taffy: "You'd never manage it George. You'd better still take yourself in hand."

Hutch: "We're not going to have one of those discussions on masturbation again."

George threw his book down and stormed outside, commenting that we were all a shower of fooking bastards.

Tom; "Now what's wrong with him?"

Johnny: "Something went wrong with his love life. He told me some time ago he was having trouble with his girlfriend. I understand his parents wanted him to marry before he came abroad. He's still supposed to be engaged but he hasn't heard from her or his own parents for a long time and he's getting edgy. He's a moody bloke and I for one will be glad when his transfer comes through. He told me his folks are pretty wealthy and had pulled strings to get him a commission but in the past few months he's become an introvert and prefers to be on his own."

Taffy: "I told you George wouldn't be able to manage a bint."

Hutch: "You know Taffy, those that boast are usually the ones that are always last in the queue."

Bill: "If ever I meet any of you blokes in Calcutta, I'll take you into Furpoys and give you a meal, the like of which you have never experienced before."

Taffy: "I still say there's no substitute for a nice piece of crumpet."

Johnny: "You know Taffy, the only cunt around here is you."

Hutch: "I agree with you Bill, the most pleasurable bodily sensation is eating and drinking, whilst copulating comes third."

Taffy: " What's second then?"

Hutch: "Shitting, and in a nice clean lav."

And so the conversation continued well into the night.

At a morning briefing we were brought up-to-date on what had been happening around us these past few weeks. We were outnumbered by the enemy, forty to one and our position was expected to become precarious. Confronting us was the Japanese 15th Army, deployed across Northern Burma and, in our sector; we were opposed by the 33rd Jap division.

There were about thirty thousand men in a Jap division, compared with our own divisional strength of less than nine thousand, most of whom were Indian Army troops. There were at least five Jap divisions in Burma. We were officially attached to the 20th Indian division who were very thin on the ground, spread out across the Kabaw valley from Tamu south to the Chindwin and beyond. It was impossible to defend several hundred square miles of jungle with such a small force and the enemy infiltrated in all directions. They had been getting through the jungle in places thought to be impassable and had carried out a number of encircling movements. Our own intelligence units hadn't been able to keep up with them. We were warned to expect to see a Jap behind every tree or bush and they didn't take prisoners. We had been taught how to kill and knew the Japs will do the same to us given the chance. The main difference between us seemed to be that we didn't seek danger and did our best to keep out of trouble. The Japs seemed only to want to commit harakiri. Orders to move over the hills into the Kabaw valley were expected as soon as the jeep track became passable.

There had been large concentrations of the enemy on the Tiddim front and our sister battery had seen action. One such action was when they managed to winch a 5.5-inch medium gun up to the summit or a hill known as Kennedy Peak. At about 8,000 feet above sea level, they claimed this to be the highest point in the world from which a medium gun had been fired. With the aid of three Willey jeeps they dismantled the gun and winched the parts up the hill, assembled it and fired on the unsuspecting Japs below.

The enemy had no gun capable of returning the fire at that time and the action inflicted severe casualties on the enemy no doubt helping to slow their advance. After the action, the gun was dismantled, lowered down the hill, reassembled and towed away. Unfortunately, when taking a bend on the narrow jeep track, which was still waterlogged, it gave way under the weight of the matador and the gun spilled over the side where there was a sheer drop of a thousand feet. Lofty Smith was the sergeant in charge and we were grieved to learn that he and his gun crew were all killed. Our O.C. wanted to ensure that a similar accident didn't happen to us; hence we were in no hurry to move just yet.

One evening we were in our usual places in the basha discussing the loss of Lofty amongst other things, when the conversation turned to Bill's whiskey supply. When asked where he obtained it, he relented and exclaimed:

"Jesus, you'll all be at it if you knew! I will give you a clue though. Remember the two New Zealanders in the R.A.F. who used to come to the mess in Quetta? Well, I met them on the Palel airstrip a few weeks ago and they obliged me with a couple of bottles."

Hutch asked: "Are they stationed there then Q?"

" I believe so, they've got a few Lysanders, you know, the dive bombers, but there wasn't much evidence the last time I was over there. Tell you what, if I see them again, I'll see if I can get some extra. Although I expect they'll be busy once this bloody rain stops."

The loss of Lofty brought to mind many men we had known during the war and inevitably, the talk lead to women and food.

Said Tom: "Remember that bint I used to cart around at Hitchin? I don't think many of you chaps ever met her but she was a lovely girl, an only daughter, her people were so friendly. I spent all my spare time at their house, including weekends. At no time did I take the girl seriously, and all I really wanted was to get my feet under their table, as the saying goes. Well, one Sunday they started to plan an engagement party. They were going to make over to me one of their houses. They even took me to see the house and confronted me with the embarrassment of choosing new wallpapers and furnishings. Up till then, I'd just played around and not taken the girl seriously. We went to the local flicks occasionally, but all I wanted was a good feed and an easy chair. The weekends I went home to see the wife. She thought I was on duty, and as you know, as my home is in Norfolk, it was too far for casual jaunts. The girl never suspected I was married and had two kids and the wife never suspected anything either, thank goodness. Funny thing, I was always going to tell her I was married and to share my two kids with her. But you know how it was, I never got round to it."

"How did you end it Tom?" I asked.

"Well, it sort of died a natural death really, the engagement party was all arranged for the weekend after we left Hitchin for the boat, the move was only just in time."

"You left her holding the baby, as it were." suggested Johnny.

"No, I can honestly say I never touched her. That is, sex wise. She was too nice a girl for that. I have had several letters from her since, forwarded on, but I've never acknowledged any of them. Haven't heard anything now for over a year. It was touch and go at the time, I can tell you. Had our embarkation been delayed I would have been in the shit. Honestly though, had it been easier for me to get home, I wouldn't have bothered about the girl."

"Having wallowed in nostalgia Tom, would you do the same thing all over again?"

"I've often thought about it. Queer thing life, everything can change by just crossing over to the other side of the road too soon or too late, if you know what I mean. I know I should have laid her. God knows I had plenty of opportunities. I'm sure I missed out there. Matter of fact I could do with her now, or any bit of crumpet for that matter."

"Who couldn't?" agreed Johnny. "You've a lot of catching up to do when this bloody war's over."

Which was a clue to Bill Lowe who, we thought, was asleep on his cot and who now started singing "When this bloody war is over" to the tune of a well known hymn. He had been secretly drinking again.

Hutch, who was lying on a blanket in the open doorway trying to read, suddenly came to life and shouted "shut that stupid row Bill or you'll find yourself outside", which was all Bill needed to shut him up and he promptly settled down to sleep again.

"If you ask me" said Hutch " and no one ever does, I would recommend to everyone to grab what they can when the opportunity arose. Life's too short to be considerate and opportunities don't come often. I'm sure most of us wish we had done something different to what we actually did. The choice is always ours but most of us have this failing of making decisions on humanitarian principles, and missing out on the risqué experiences. I've always thought that the females I've been involved with have been dirty bitches and only meant for bedding down, but perhaps I mixed with the wrong type. I agree with you though Tom. I would rather have a bit of crumpet right now, than bloody read about it."

Johnny said: "It'll be two years since we left England, I wonder how much longer it will be before we are able to get back home?"

To that, there was no answer.

We didn't know it then, but this was the last time we would all be together, under one roof. Our conversation was not always about sex and food. That morning I had collected a bag of mail. My wife had sent me the latest photos of my two children. My son, who had just had his third birthday, was seen sitting astride a toy tricycle, whilst my daughter, who I had not yet seen, appeared to be a blonde and with a lovely smile. She was dressed up in mother's shoes, hat, and fox fur. I wanted to weep when I first saw the photos and couldn't resist the opportunity of showing off and handing the pictures around. Tom and I were the only ones present who could boast of a family.

"My boy, who's the eldest, is now ten and writes to me when the wife reminds him. He reckons he's joining the R.A.F. when he's old enough so he can join me out here." said Tom.

"That doesn't say much for our chances Tom, when you think about it. It could be a very long time before we see them again. Or should we be pessimistic and say if?"

"I don't know, with all this talk of a second front and the Yanks throwing their weight about, it's gonna shorten the war, trouble is, the bloody war out here hasn't really started yet." Hutch said.

"What will you do when you get back to Civvy Street Hutch?" I asked.

"I don't know, I've never had a job, and have no ambition to accumulate money. After all, my folks have plenty of loot, a lot more, in fact, than they'll ever need, so why should I worry? I will certainly resist becoming a 'nine-to-five' automaton and developing ulcers in trying to keep up with the Jones, you know, a new car every year, even if it means going without other things. I might try the Colonial Service. I have relatives in the Foreign Office; I'm certainly not working for a living. After all, why work? I don't intend to marry, and I've always been on the side of the underdog. I'll even support the miners every time they go on strike," said Hutch.

"Balls! I don't agree with you there, Hutch." Said Tom. "The bloody miners have been on strike again, sodding up the war effort and it's those bastards who should be sent out here to do their share."

Hutch responded. "Fuck off! Why shouldn't they take advantage of the situation? Lots of people are making money out of the war, a lot of money at that, and, unfortunately there's nothing you or I can do about it. We all know that money is a god and can be bought and sold. There will always be rich and poor, war or no war, but the fact that there is a war means a lot of greedy sods will take advantage of it. Alright, take the miners, wasn't it Churchill who was quoted as saying that England was built on coal and surrounded by fish? And a little extra effort would solve all the country's problems? And who benefits? Not the miners or the fishermen, I can assure you. We all know what happened to the coal, the miners refused to win too much, as they feared too much stock at the pit head would limit their bargaining power. So, whilst money is a more important commodity than coal, the requisite mental outlook for prosperity does not exist. Now you've got me wound up. Do you know that ever since Victorian times when the public schools were first established, there has been a bias towards middle class culture, which has remained antipathetic towards industry and industrial progress? Do you know that State education was opposed by the Victorian liberals, as they didn't want a classless society? Otherwise money wouldn't mean anything. In those days society was content to churn out Christian gentlemen who's main task was to govern the Empire, and they've been doing it ever since. And if I can find myself a suitable niche in a warm climate, that's exactly what I intend to do. I don't want to get mixed up with commerce as I can see trouble when the ordinary laborer becomes better educated. He'll query why he should dirty his hands when those with money are able to live off him like leeches." It was unusual for Hutch to be so eloquent.

The discussion then went on to leeches and sores and other complaints but what was said was soon forgotten. We were all caught in a web that engulfed us and we would be lucky to survive. So far we hadn't seen any of the Japs with the protruding teeth as depicted on the war propaganda. But those we had seen were small; trouble was they were so numerous. We dreaded the thought of meeting them and engaging in hand-to-hand combat, which now seemed probable. We were reminded of the havoc caused when a stores tent collapsed at Bangalore, under the weight of a termites nest between the roof and the outer flysheet. There were hundreds of thousands of the yellow insects and we didn't know they were there. We hoped the Japs made their presence known. That evening we had a stand-to and orders were issued to move into the battle zone.

FIFTEEN

AT FIRST LIGHT we said goodbye to George McWilliams as transport took him back to Imphal. We were sorry to lose him. He had volunteered for the commandos and was posted back to India. We would never see him again.

We assembled on the road at 0700 hours, ready to move off, destination Tamu, south into Burma. The echelon section of fifteen vehicles followed me in the jeep, the battery captain leading. The R.H.Q. contingent had started fifteen minutes earlier and the guns would follow at a reasonable interval. All traffic today was one way, south.

It was an easy ride on the macadam road to the first foothills. At the end of the sealed road a track had been cut into the hillside that narrowed as it climbed, winding it's way up the side of the first hill to about 1,000 feet. Here we had a magnificent panorama, under a clear blue sky the jungle covered hills were lush and brilliant green after the heavy rains. After a short halt to admire the view and allow the following convoy to catch up, round a sharp bend the track suddenly dropped out of sight. The sun had not yet penetrated to this side of the hill and yellow mud a foot deep and as slippery as an ice rink caused the jeep and trailer to slide several hundred feet before coming to halt beside our battery captain's 15 hundred weight truck that was stuck fast.

To give you some idea of the typography of the area, a range of hills separates the Imphal plain from the Kabaw valley. The hills are steep and precipitous and climb about 3,000 feet. The valleys contain hidden swamps and rivers. To complicate matters, the contour of the hills is from northeast to southwest whereas our journey was from north to south. Consequently, the track had been carved into the sides of the hills using age-old mule tracks, up and down, around and around and in some instances over the top of some hills. Where the monsoon rains had washed away large sections of the track, hasty repairs had been carried out and in many instances, a new track prepared. But lack of metal and constant use by thousands of boots and hooves had left a soft yellow muddy surface that became very dangerous. We radioed back to the convoy to fit chains and with much swearing and digging managed to resume the journey, in bottom gear.

It was a hair raising experience, negotiating impossible hillocks, and often losing control. Towards evening we reached the last summit from which we looked down on the Kabaw valley. Here, some distance south, was the River Chindwin and the enemy.

The last slide was known as Chocolate Hill and would be impossible to use in the wet season. There is no doubt that this natural obstacle was the ultimate defense. The depth of the impenetrable hills was the contributing factor in preventing the Japanese from capturing the Imphal area, the gateway to India, at least for now.

The valley floor was not as flat as our maps indicated and the convoy was soon lost in the dense undergrowth. We followed a well-established track of yellow mud. On each side was a wall of thick jungle. We were soon engulfed. It was claustrophobic.

The track followed the easiest contour, skirting huge clumps of bamboo, tree stumps and other immovable growth until at last we arrived at a crossroads. Here we met traffic controllers who directed us to our destination. There were new traffic signs everywhere through the maze of tracks that branched off in all directions. At walking pace we avoided holes of liquid mud, hidden obstacles and fallen trees and eventually arrived at the place that was to be our wagon lines. Here the vehicles were hidden in the jungle undergrowth and we began to dig in. We had been instructed to leave all our Indian followers behind and I was delighted when my store man informed me that five of them had refused to go and were in the cookhouse wagon. These chaps were very keen and good workers, so as soon as they were finished with the cookhouse, they helped with the digging.

My first job was to search for water as the water wagon had traveled empty. Taking my store man I went off to find the guns, with a hot meal packed in vacuum flasks. Because of the distance between Tamu and the gun position near Sittaung on the Chindwin, the Matador tractors and other vehicles were retained with the guns, in case they had to make a hasty move. This was the only occasion where the battery was divided, as artillery support was necessary to a forward box. In other wars, gunnery experience dictated that the normal position of the wagon lines was well away from danger. We were taught that it was normal practice for the infantry to be the first to make contact with the enemy, whilst artillery supported them at a safe distance in the rear. Wagon lines were at an even safer distance away from the guns. But this was not like any other war. Here, every fighting group had to be contained in a 'Box' capable of being defended on all sides and supplied by air. The well-worn track was not too difficult to follow as it made its way over riverbeds. Engineers had cut paths down the thirty-foot high riverbanks and covered the jungle floor with logs and bamboo mats. It took a lot of concentration to get there and back in daylight.

During the next few weeks I followed the same wheel marks from the wagon lines to the guns and back, through a tunnel of dense jungle, never meeting another living soul. Jolts from hidden rocks and roots were unavoidable at any speed and the jungle growth seemed to get denser each day as it strived to recover the space made vacant by the passage of vehicles. Protruding branches and huge tropical leaves clawed at me, as the jeep had no hood or windscreen. I spent many hours each day travel-ing this track, suffering the monotony but at the same time keeping alert to the hidden peril just around the next corner. To relieve the tedium, I often recited nursery rhymes or poetry. I recited the 23rd Psalm in full, many times. The sentence that began "though I walk through the valley of death," haunted me and I hoped this was not an omen. A slit trench in the wagon lines was my home, where I felt secure and my fears evaporated.

I hadn't seen Tom for several days and it didn't occur to me that he was missing from the gun site, until one day we met as he came up from the underground command post. We exchanged greetings and he told me he had been out with the old man for a few days on one of his walks. The O.C. liked to go out on his own for the day into the jungle on a sort of lone patrol. However if he stayed out at night, he took someone with him. One day he told Tom they were going for a long walk for maybe two or three days, that he should bring rations, packs and a groundsheet and arms. When they stumbled across a village they kept at a safe distance, concealed in the undergrowth, they watched women and children doing their laundry. As they watched through field glasses they saw about two dozen enemy on the other side of the pool watching and taking no precautions to conceal themselves. Tom wanted to get out of there quickly but the old man wanted to wait until it was safe. He would often collect useful information of enemy movements on his jaunts.

I was driving back from the guns one evening when, after crossing a dried up river and climbing the opposite bank at speed I was confronted by a huge elephant. It roared and reared up on its rear legs and looked like it would crush the jeep and me. I sounded my horn and yelled back. It made off through the undergrowth and several others followed him, stampeding and crashing their way through the jungle until they were out of sight. This encounter put the fear of god into me. The jeep stalled. I could not get it to start for ages. I wanted to get out of there in case they returned. And I thought it would be a great place for an ambush. I reported this to H.Q. We had been warned that a number of elephants had wandered off from the logging mill some miles north.

On other occasions crossing the dried up river I often confronted strange white birds. They had a long neck and extra large legs. They seemed large enough to lift me out of my drivers seat and into the air, with wingspans of at least ten feet. I could never find anyone to positively identify the bird.

Despite all the precautions we took there was an outbreak of diarrhea that developed into dysentery. There was little we could do about it. There was no relief from the plague of flies and mosquitoes. With the shortage of water and the fine yellow dust that stuck to everything, it was impossible to tell who was jaundiced or who hadn't washed.

In preparation for the coming offensive, the authorities issued fourteen days of American K rations for use in emergency, should normal rations not be available. One day's K ration consisted of three meals, breakfast, lunch and dinner. Each had a separate flat package with the days rations enclosed in a waterproof cardboard box. Each meal had a number of small packages and cans with many items dehydrated with instructions on how to cook them. There was great variety so it was always fun to open a package and compare it to the man next to you. In each meal were two American cigarettes, candles, chocolate and toilet paper. Some packages had toothpaste or hair cream or a message from the packer. The variety intrigued us.

I took two vehicles and six men to the specified issue point and collected enough rations for the entire regiment, understanding that the authorities were never wrong. After R.H.Q. had their share, we were left with double our entitlement. From then on I took a larger vehicle on a daily jaunt to the guns and distributed the K rations. Our O.C. was delighted when I told him of our luck with the extra rations and the men were jubilant when some were distributed as a bonus.

Driving back from the wagon lines one evening we were waved down by a Gurkha patrol. A few days before, orders had been received from Division that due to enemy infiltration in our area, no one was allowed to be on any road or track unless in a convoy consisting of at least five vehicles and twenty four men. We didn't think this order was for us. However the Gurkha sergeant asked us to step down from the cab. He then searched the truck aided by several other Gurkhas who suddenly appeared.

Fifty yards down the track was another vehicle which had been ransacked and everything portable taken. The driver sat in the driver's seat with his head to one side and his eyes staring into space. Another private was dead in the bushes. Both men had been bayoneted to death. I had never seen so much blood. The Gurkhas were afraid the vehicle was booby-trapped but it wasn't so one of them drove it back to Tamu. From that day on, I only traveled in convoy.

We all had our private part of a trench and I spent my nights counting the stars and wishing the war would end. Sleep was continuously disturbed by gunfire.

The morning after our guns had supported forward infantry, I sensed something was amiss as soon as I arrived on the gun site. A shell had exploded inside the barrel of one of the guns and the end of the barrel was splayed out, like a flower in bloom. Shrapnel from the explosion had killed one man and severely wounded four others but by the time I arrived the wounded had been evacuated. There seemed to be more concern about one gun than the wounded and it couldn't be left as it was, as the chances of a replacement was nil. The gun with crew had to proceed to the main engineering workshops in Imphal to get the barrel shortened. The crew followed me back to the wagon lines. The theory about the breech explosion was that the amatol filling in the shell had liquefied in the intense heat of the sun and the sudden shock had acted as a fuse, exploding the shell before it left the barrel. A few days after this incident the guns were brought back from their advanced position and dug in about half a mile from the wagon lines, commanding the main track south and dominating the improvised airstrip near Tamu.

With a brigade of the 20th Division, we were now in a defensive box that we expected to defend against all attacks, being supplied by air if necessary. The guns were about ten minutes away, down the track.

A large concentration of Japs was making their way slowly through the jungle to the east of us but we couldn't do anything about it. In our sector we could easily be surrounded, but the enemy made no move. We had to be prepared to defend our position from all directions and we were now imprisoned by barbed wire.

Because of the breech explosion and the fact that we were in a confined space, it was decided to unload all our spare ammunition and bury it. The only logical place was back along the road in the foothills. Small batches of shells were stacked in cut out caves by the roadside and the earth allowed to bury them. The task took several days and I went along with the fatigue party when we came under shellfire. The Japs were using 105 mm guns that seemed to have a longer range than anything we had. We were warned about drainage trenches being booby-trapped. We lost a man that day. We were in an exposed position several hundred feet up when we heard the first shell approaching. The whine was of such a note that I could tell it was going to fall at a distance from us and we watched it explode lower down the hill. The next shell sounded much nearer and the whine became louder. We all dropped to the ground automatically. All that is, except one man who dived into the drainage trench by his side. The trench was booby-trapped. He received the full force of the explosion in his lower regions. His body muffled the detonation and it was hard to believe he was in serious trouble. I helped him out onto the road and as I lifted him, his intestines spilled out. Despite being stripped to the waist like the rest of us, his body was on fire. The blood and stench from the open wound nauseated me and it annoyed me when the men crowded around. He began to cry like a baby and tried to tell me something but there was nothing we could do for him. I injected the contents of a phial of morphine into him and hoped it was the correct thing to do. Wrapping him in a blanket we made haste to the first aid station but he was dead before we arrived.

This was one of many tragedies I would witness. It annoyed me that some men expressed malicious pleasure in other's misfortunes, as they did on this occasion. Then there was always one man, who to satisfy his curiosity would vomit at the sight of so much blood and guts. This would set off a chain reaction. The odor of death would linger for days.

Two things happened about this time, our O.C. was suddenly posted back to England and would have something to do with the second front, and news came that George McWilliams had been killed. He never got to India. He joined an assault unit of the commandos and was in an abortive seaborne landing near the port of Akyab on the Arakan front. Apparently the landing barge was blown up when it struck a Jap mine and all hands were lost.

As the enemy closed in, we constructed defenses and cleared the jungle around the wagon lines. We now had a system of slit trenches. No one was above ground unless on duty. We watched and listened. A lorry starting up or a battery charger brought in to play, shattered the silence, but any noise was disapproved of. Men tended to speak softly and an atmosphere of nervous expectancy prevailed. With no wind, the stillness accentuated the odor of rotting vegetation and human excrement. The yellow dust filtered the sun's rays. And the earth was scorched in the relentless sunshine as we perspired with no opportunity to wash or change our clothing.

The yellow dust permeated everything. Dust was several inches deep on the track and splashed like water when trodden on. A fine film had penetrated our skin and clothing so that we blended in with the surroundings.

Other units were near us in our box but were well concealed and we seldom saw or heard them. The enemy was in Kelewa on the Chindwin that was only a day's march from us. They were there in strength, so it became an exciting expedition every time one emptied one's bowels in the jungle.

An occasional convoy from Imphal would bring fresh troops, food and supplies and sometimes mail. All the food was tinned so although we wanted to conserve our K rations we couldn't resist occasionally breaking open a new box. We received instructions as to what to do if we were over-run and we managed to survive, but we couldn't believe this would ever happen to us. Surviving that is, not being over-run.

One morning Johnny and Hutch came over from R.H.Q. to see me and I was shocked when they told me all the R.H.Q. staff had been ordered back to Imphal. They acted as if they were going on leave, as they would soon be out of the danger zone. I was happy for them, although I was sorry to see them go. I daresay, given the same chance, I would have gone with them. Even so, I believe Johnny was torn between the desire to escape or remain with men he had known for so long. Several of our chaps went back with them for hospital treatment. Rumors were rife that we also would be sent back, as our guns were much too valuable to sacrifice. But our hopes in this direction were shattered when we heard of the panic to recover the gun that had been sent to get its muzzle shortened.

The gun was still in the Royal Electrical and Mechanical Engineers (R.E.M.E.) workshops in Imphal, and the top brass were very distressed that it wasn't in action yet. We heard that the entire R.E.M.E. staff had been threatened to be transferred to an active infantry battalion should the gun not be with us within 48 hours. Of course the gun arrived on time and proved invaluable in the days to come. It took up a position at the end of the temporary airstrip for use as an anti-tank weapon.

It was reported the Japs had heavy tanks nearby but we couldn't believe they had found a way of getting them across the Chindwin River. As if to confirm this report several Lee Grant tanks arrived and parked nearby, shattering our peace and creating more dust.

I had always dreaded the thought of suddenly being confronted with a choice of life or death, kill or be killed. I've never fancied the idea of sticking a bayonet into another living person, or for that matter to be on the receiving end and that is why I chose a Sten gun. I always had it with me. A few months previously I would have thought it highly improbable to have to make such a decision but not any more. I was now conditioned and the sooner we killed the Japs, the sooner we could return home.

One morning, when I was down in the command post on the gun

position, I overheard a conversation regarding an ordnance dump nearby which was to be destroyed. There appeared to be some urgency and doubt as to whether army engineers would have enough time to blow it up or if it should be left to our gunners. Apparently, the dump had been prepared many months ago as a reserve for the eventual advance on Rangoon but it had now become an embarrassment. I ascertained the dump was situated at a distance from the base of Chocolate Hill, at the end of a road army engineers had been preparing, but had now abandoned. I told Tom about it and suggested we should see if there was anything useful there. Quite frankly, I didn't suggest this out of bravado; I was bored to tears with nothing to do. So early next morning I took Bill Lowe with me to find the dump. We discovered the new road rough cut out of the jungle and followed it.

SIXTEEN

MONSOON RAINS HAD taken its toll. Jungle growth had started to obliterate the earthworks. Elephant grass was ten feet tall but the road was discernable. We followed a track expecting to find the dump but at the end of a more recent cutting stumbled on a lorry park. The comment from Bill was "Jesus!" Scattered around the clearing were several bulldozers and tractors and it looked as if they had been abandoned in haste. The whole area was deserted.

We toured around and found a clearing once used as a campsite and at another clearing found a row of lorries parked wheel to wheel. There were twenty trucks, all six wheeled Studebakers with low reduction gears, ideal for these tracks. "Jesus!" Bill exclaimed again. "I don't believe they've just left this lot to rot and just pissed off. Look at them Q. They must be nearly new. Hold on, let's have a look." And without hesitation, but checking for booby traps, Bill got behind the wheel and I stepped into the passenger seat. We lit cigarettes. All was quiet.

"What puzzles me," I said. "Is why these have been left here to rot? They must have been here for a long time and I wonder anyone will collect them."

"It's another example of how quickly they can waste their money Q. It makes me sick. This fucking lot must be worth a fortune. Wish we could get some of them back up to Calcutta. Wonder if we could get one to work?"

When we got the bonnet open, we found the engine still held oil and water but we didn't know how to start it or if anything was wrong so we dismounted and continued our search for the dump. We walked down several tracks, some of which criss-crossed at various points until we came to a much-used track that we followed. It came to a large clearing and there neatly stacked and covered in tarpaulins and camouflage nets, was the dump. There were several stacks of forty-gallon drums of oil and two gallon cans of petrol together with neat stacks of large wooden boxes.

Several Indian privates were sitting under a tarpaulin watching us as we were about to break open a box, when a Corporal sauntered over and started shouting and waving his rifle about. Soon, half a dozen Indian privates had woken up and approached us, followed by a Jemadar who demanded to see our authority. He spoke English and we lied, telling him we wanted to inspect the site before we brought in the demolition team. He was quite friendly and conducted us around the dump. He had an idea what each dump contained and we wished we had some chalk to mark the mounds of stores that would be worth taking away. He seemed satisfied with our explanation and we promised to see him again in a few days.

Back at base, and thinking about our discovery at stand-to, I had my doubts if we would get any lorries working as this would be essential if we raided the dump. There was no spare room on our transport. We could always find use for tarpaulins and camouflage nets and perhaps a few cans of petrol.

Next morning I got Bill to spread the word of our discovery and to find out whether our motor engineers had any ideas about Studebakers. Almost every man volunteered for the raiding party.

Later that morning, Bill escorted four motor mechanics to the truck park and by late afternoon they were back at the wagon lines with a Studebaker in working order. They also brought back several engine parts and batteries that were put on charge. The problem was our battery charging plant made a lot of noise and could be heard miles away but since the few tanks nearby were often running their engines, we didn't think our noise would matter much. Thinking of the enormity of the task of bringing down the Studebakers and raiding the dump, I told Tom what we intended to do and asked him to sound out the C.O. We didn't want to be mistaken for an enemy force, if we made the raid.

During the short time we had been in our present position, our officers had been taking turns to fly with the R.A.F. acting as Observation Posts (O.P.s). They had used the forward airstrip just in front of our gun position and were using old R.A.F. biplanes. The last thing we needed at this stage was to have an enthusiastic O.P. officer giving instructions to shell us. However no one wanted to take responsibility for what we had in mind and to dampen my enthusiasm, the C.O. ordered me to stand by and be ready to move at a moments notice as things were heating up. Meanwhile Bill informed me that the mechanics had been successful in getting five Studebakers to work and that they had been left in the vehicle park.

We decided it was now or never so very early next morning we took the Studebaker from our lines with two-dozen men and made haste for the stores dump, collecting the other five trucks on the way. We were all excited and from the dust we created you would think the entire army was on the move. I had expected an awkward situation to develop if there was any opposition to our raid but when we arrived, the dump was deserted. We found wooden cases full of bottles of limejuice, a mound of tinned Woodbine cigarettes and several cases of rum in bottles. I took charge of a large cask of rum and thought what a great party we could have. We took all the two-gallon cans of petrol we had room for plus many tarpaulins and camouflage nets. One useful find was a large container of anti-mosquito cream, made in Hollywood. I wondered how it got there and if it was intended for army use. We found this invaluable during the weeks to come.

The six additional lorries were parked out of sight in the jungle near our wagon lines and drivers were allocated in case we moved quickly. Two days after the raid, army engineers demolished the dump. What a terrible waste that was.

As the enemy drew closer and as our guns were in such close proximity, we were called to stand-to constantly. During the night machine gun fire and grenade explosions could be heard, sometimes faraway to the south or nearer to hand. The sound would ricochet across the valley. We witnessed the Very lights and gun flashes similar to distant summer lightning. The action was getting closer by the hour. It would soon be our turn. Until the moon rose, the stars shone with a new brilliance as if to mock us. We were warned again and again to be on continuous alert and be ready to move at a moments notice.

The 20th Indian Division had an impossible task of defending a front of more than 250 miles in this sector of Northern Burma. The brigade, that we were attached to, occupied several boxes across the most accessible route. Each 'box' was named, but names matter not, what was important was that the enemy thrust had been slowed and they were suffering heavy casualties. All the action was confined to the forward units of the brigade who were slowly retreating towards us. Our position in the wagon lines did not have enough barbed wire. There was none available. Concern was for the large number of men who wandered about at night to relieve themselves and who suffered in silence from the pangs of dysentery. It was feared a situation would develop where men would shoot at anything moving after dark and our own men would be victims. Many new recruits were already sick with dysentery. The younger men seemed more susceptible to the disease. There was no treatment available and the sick had to be left to their own devices. I hoped the limejuice would help and I told the men to help themselves. Mac discovered three cases of bottled rum in a Studebaker and he took these under his control. I wondered if all the rum had been accounted for, but didn't pursue the matter.

As we entered a new phase of the battle, all enthusiasm was knocked out of us and we snatched odd moments of rest after sleepless nights. After several weeks, some men had lost weight. Dysentery had caused the loss of some men's legs and they had to be assisted to move about. Some never came out of their foxholes.

Our guns were in action one morning, an hour before dawn. This interrupted my enjoyable dream. I was back as a schoolboy standing over an open basement grating of the bakers shop opposite the house where I was born, savoring the sweet smell of fresh crusty bread and wallowing in the heat from the grating on a cold winter's day. Then the guns fired again. The concussion left us in a stupor and the jolt on the nervous system left us in awe, trembling. Men opened their mouths wide to lessen the effect of the shock waves. The little plastic earplugs issued months ago had been lost or destroyed. Laying in my foxhole the noise reverberated and dirt fell on my face. Dust began to rise everywhere and we didn't need orders to stand-to. The nerve-wracking sound of explosions, the whiplash of the guns and the rattle of machine guns ceased as suddenly as it had started. The ultimate silence was even more pronounced. In the half-light you imagined movement in the jungle and there was a strong temptation to fire a few rounds just to see whether the shadows were real. But we held our fire.

One night, the silence was broken by a large fleet of planes. When they came into view, shining in the moonlight, we saw each plane was towing a glider. There was a repeat performance the following night and we learned this was the airborne division of the Chindits led by General Orde Wingate on their way to central Burma, several hundred miles behind enemy lines. We were reminded of the scheme to dismantle one of our guns and pack it into a Dakota transport plane. Several demonstrations proved it was impracticable to take the gun by air, reassemble it and fire a round. Otherwise we would have been up there with those poor devils. The chances of returning alive from that expedition were less than 50-50, as was subsequently proved.

News that the enemy had reached Kohima, 250 miles to our rear and that the road into India was closed, wasn't very reassuring. Our troops in that area had been fighting a losing battle. The Japs had secretly built bunkers and roadblocks all over the place and bitter fighting was taking place. We couldn't expect any further supplies in the near future.

General Slim stated that this was good news as it would be easier to kill more Japs as they closed in on us.

In our sector, battalions of enemy infantry had been seen marching in formation, accompanied by several heavy tanks. They were only five miles away and we could expect an attack in considerable strength at any hour. We could only sit and wait. Soon after dark we started firing our battery of 25-pounders to support the forward infantry. The whiplash and concussion of the guns shut out all other noises. We kept below ground as the enemy returned fire. Red tracer bullets ricocheted off the trees over our heads and it was impossible to determine where the firing was coming from. We remained below ground and held our fire. It felt like we were surrounded by the entire Japanese Army and hoped that we wouldn't have to face them up close.

Early next morning Tom came over to the wagon lines, and in view of the situation, we made arrangements to collect all the ammunition we had previously buried on the track back towards Palel, so we could be mobile when necessary. There was a full moon and the operation was to be carried out that same night. Mac provided tea and as we talked, the Lee Grant tanks parked nearby started their engines and moved off down towards the guns. We were pleased to see them go.

The military situation was now far more serious. The infantry had fallen back and were now within sight of our gunners. There had been an exchange of small arms fire during the night, but, so far, no major attack. Although I had thought Tom had come down for a spot of rum and put me in the picture regarding our possible early move, I sensed there was something else troubling him and urged him to come clean.

"I don't know how to tell you this 'Q'", he said, "but you'll get to know the sad news eventually, so I thought it best to see you myself."

"What's happened?" I asked.

"You've lost your mate. You'd better sit down and let's open a bottle, the old man had a phone call early this morning with the news that R.H.Q., had been wiped out. The only survivor was the store man and he happened to be sleeping on the ground between stacks of cases of bully beef. The Japs made an early morning raid and dropped their bombs across R.H.Q.'s camp. Apparently they were asleep in tents, although they had planned to dig-in, they hadn't yet got around to it. They all died instantly and couldn't have known what hit them. Twenty-three are dead they told him, including Johnny and Hutch."

Grief overcame me, my heart missed a beat and I wanted to give way to emotion. "The bastards." I whispered. "I remember accusing Johnny of wanting to piss off to escape the fighting, he didn't want to go you know."

"Have you got the home addresses of Johnny and Hutch?" asked Tom. "I've got Johnny's and will write to his wife when we can get mail out. I've no idea of Hutch's address."

"By the way, we're still on full alert and should be able to move at a moments notice, so keep everyone on their toes."

"Did you know one of our drivers died during the night, another mystery. He appeared to be alright yesterday, so they tell me, so will you get permission to bury the poor sod?"

"Look Q, I've got to get back, thanks for the drink and be ready to move, it'll be in a fucking hurry I can tell you."

I now began to realize just how critical our present situation had become. So far we had escaped the fighting and the fact that we had to be prepared to move indicated we were not going to be sacrificed after all. In moments of adversity I have been amazed how swiftly we react to self-preservation and yet during an attack, we are convinced we will not be killed this time.

During the night Tom phoned from the gun site and told me they were in the thick of it. They had exchanged small arms fire when the Japs tried to get at the guns, but, thanks to the Gurkhas, the attack had been repulsed. He confirmed once more that orders were that we were to be ready to move off at first light. He expressed fears that we at the wagon lines were in the middle of a battle, as all the noise seemed to come from our end. He said he would confirm the timing of the move at daybreak but the battle continued all the next day and into the night and it would have been disastrous to attempt to move. It was about three a.m. and very dark, when movement orders eventually came. I dispatched the Matadors to collect the guns and I followed our wagon lines officer to the new position.

SEVENTEEN

THE MOVE WAS carried out at speed. Even the sick came to life and co-operated. We were all glad to move away from the foulness, the disgusting stench and the dust. If the Japs wanted that territory they were welcome to it. The new site was cramped for space but dust free and slightly elevated above the level of the Kabaw valley. Thick growth prevented a view of the valley but it was a delightful spot with bush-covered hills to the north, rising to about five hundred feet and reminiscent of a favorite part of Devon. Everyone dug frantically, gun pits, pits for ammunition and petrol. Slit trenches and foxholes took shape. Some holes were close together but this was unavoidable.

I hadn't paid much attention to Mac my store man and as we worked we talked. I think he wanted to take my mind off the loss of Johnny. Mac had been my store man for three years and I had ignored him and taken him for granted as everything had run smoothly. His name was Ted McDermot, but everyone called him Mac.

It often happened in the army that a man became known by a nickname and his real name was never known. He lived with his wife and two children in Somerset. At the outbreak of war he was a member of the Territorial Army and, had it not been for that, he wouldn't now be in the army as his occupation of farm worker was reserved. He was very honest, a good mechanic and as strong as an ox. In fact, I don't think there was anyone of the same caliber in our unit. Mac chose a spot for our sleeping quarters under a large clump of bamboo and commenced digging, whilst I supervised our five followers to dig a pit large enough to take several dozen boxes of charges. By the end of the third day all defenses were completed.

During this time the enemy shelled the vacated gun site where engineers had laid thunder flashes, timed to detonate at intervals over three days. This proved invaluable as our infantry ambushed a large raiding party there after the vacated position had been under bombardment. And our own gunners were able to carry out counter battery fire. Firepower was directed by an officer flying in an R.A.F. Lysander, acting as O.P. It was possible that some enemy guns were silenced as the shelling fizzled out. But the Lysander and crew were shot down, and this was the last aircraft available to us. Two other planes had been lost over enemy lines during the previous few weeks and now we were three officers short.

We had just settled down in our new surroundings when the enemy attacked in considerable strength using tanks. Our gun with the sawn off barrel was sent forward and used as an anti-tank gun. It took up a position under supervision of the tank commander. An infantry company supported the volunteer crew. Firing over open sights, our gunners destroyed the leading tank but the column was held whilst other enemy tanks tried to negotiate the difficult terrain but without success. Meanwhile our battery fired into the tank and infantry concentration and inflicted severe casualties. It was later revealed that the Jap infantry employed in this attack were from the Imperial Guard. With fanatical courage they made several attempts to rush and destroy our sawn-off gun but our own tanks held them and cleared the area. The gun was pulled out after dark and returned to the safety of the gun site. We had no casualties.

We heard our Lee Grant tanks move south early next morning and there was much machine-gunning all that day. None of our tanks returned and there were a number of fires burning during the night. The situation then followed an established pattern in that the enemy gave up the idea of further frontal attacks for the time being and began to infiltrate all round the brigade position, probing, mostly at night. They got perilously close to our position and we frequently came under fire and were compelled to keep below ground. During a lull in the fighting, one morning, two of our men stood smoking and talking when one of then collapsed and fell into the undergrowth. We recovered his body and discovered he had a bullet hole in his head. He must have died instantly. We had been warned that Jap snipers, using silencers and telescopic sights had been in operation nearby but no one took any notice until this incident. From now on we lived like rabbits, only coming up for food and water. If we had to go to the toilet, there was no privacy, as one man squatted, at least three others kept guard.

During the following night there were some casualties from enemy shelling and another man died in his sleep. We had no idea of the cause of his death, as he hadn't been sick before.

Fires burned down in the valley for several days. Smoke blocked out the sun and at night the sky was illuminated. Fine dust, mixed with the smoke came up from the valley penetrating our lungs and we wondered if the old pagodas were going up in smoke. A strong smell of cordite was in the air.

The foxhole Mac and I shared was a peculiar shape, it was the best we could do in the circumstances. We entered it by lowering ourselves down three feet to the first step, then a sharp turn to the left and down a further two steps to the bottom. Mac had cut away the roots of the bamboo and this now formed a solid roof. Slits were dug outwards for ventilation and for a lookout. Although we were pretty cramped, we were thankful for the shelter, even though we were on the extreme edge of the perimeter of the gun site. If the enemy came in our direction, we would be the first to welcome them. Within six yards of our foxhole, the followers had dug a hole about ten feet square and six feet deep and this was now full of ammunition charges in steel boxes, covered by a tarpaulin. The followers slept under this tarpaulin. Their next task was to assist in digging a command post but this was to be much larger and deep enough to stand erect in, and covered by logs then sandbagged.

We now had several days respite when our guns were not used. This was a relief as it was extremely hot. One quiet evening, during stand-to, we were enjoying a concoction Mac had cooked from K rations, had American coffee and lit Camel cigarettes. After our traditional British ration of bully beef and dog biscuits, this was a real treat. As we smoked, Mac talked about his life in Somerset. Like many others, both young and old, he was caught up in the patriotic fervor of 1938 when Chamberlain returned from Germany waving his 'peace in our time' scrap of paper signed by Adolph Hitler. Mac was conned into joining the Territorial Army with most of his village during this emotional crisis.

Sitting in our quarters, there wasn't room for even one of us to lie down. We finished our cigarettes and our thoughts turned to home and loved ones, but Mac seemed disturbed. During the uncanny silence of the jungle I could hear him scratching away at his three days growth of beard. We had decided to join the fashion and grow beards, as there were no more razor blades. I wanted very much to be alone with my thoughts. I was abrupt and moody. I was angry that the loss of Johnny had already been forgotten. Not one man was really concerned, even Tom wasn't really interested. I tried to shake off this miserable feeling and I know the remorse would persist until I'd written to Johnny's wife and told my own wife, but words escaped me. What do I tell them? That he died bravely? Johnny had died in his sleep; the top of his head had been blown off.

Next morning we had a look at the little stream, a few yards outside our perimeter but near our foxhole. A bank of about eight feet surrounded the gulley and we had to cut footholds to get down into it. It was so well concealed that we didn't see it until we were on top of it. On inspection, the gulley was about a hundred yards long and six yards wide shaped after a letter 'S' and the sandy floor had little growth. The water appeared out of the ground at one end and disappeared at the other end, and there was a trickle of water about equal to a slow running domestic water tap. We dug a hole at the side of the stream and, when it was deep enough, diverted the stream, hoping the hole would eventually fill. There was Jap air activity that afternoon but no other action and we had a reasonable night, dreaming of the bath we planned. Early next morning our peace was shattered when our guns opened fire to support our infantry and one Jap gun, thought to be a 105 mm howitzer placed several shells dangerously near.

We were now handicapped as it was impossible to maintain a conventional observation post, the nature of the terrain prevented any view of the valley. To overcome this, survey parties were put up onto the surrounding hills and, by logging enemy gun flashes from several angles, we were able to pinpoint the enemy gun positions with reasonable accuracy. The enemy had the advantage though, as they had room to move whilst we remained static.

That afternoon the hole we had dug in the gulley was full of crystal clear water so we stripped off and stepped in. We sat down carefully so as not to disturb the clearness of the water and wallowed. It was many months since we had had the pleasure of a bath and we made the most of it, using soap that had become hard and cracked. At the same time, we washed our clothes. In the midst of our ablutions we decided it would only be fair to tell the other lads of our discovery. I had had a good wash, washed my hair and underclothes and had just stepped out of the pool when a Jap fighter plane flew over, very low. It's appearance was so sudden, I froze and watched as it turned and, as it commenced to make it's way in our direction there was a mad scramble to get under cover, the plane approached at speed and as shells began to explode on the ground I dived into an old slit trench. I landed on a roll of rusted barbed wire that had been left in the trench and abandoned many months previously and, being nude, I felt a thousand pin pricks biting into my flesh.

The plane didn't return and I was glad to get out of there. Mac was lucky. He only got dirty. It was agony climbing out of that trench and when I finally alighted, I was covered in blood from the dozens of tiny punctures made by the barbed wire. We both washed down again in the pool and Mac was able to don his wet clothes but I couldn't stop the bleeding so I put on my boots and carrying my clothes, made haste to the command post. The front of my wet body was running freely with blood and I must have looked a gruesome sight to those in the command post. I was wearing only boots and a steel helmet.

The command post had two entrances and there was room for half dozen stretchers on the dirt floor. It had a radio transmitter-receiver and phone. The medical orderly cleaned me up, the little holes soon clotted and I was able to dress, but I was very sore. A score of jagged wounds were covered by plaster dressings, under my arms and on my stomach and chest and, thanks to the prompt attention of the orderly, the wounds healed quickly. Before leaving the command post I was able to don my wet clothes that cooled my fevered body. For the remainder of that day, Mac in his concern, supplied tea and cigarettes while we both relaxed in a sea of perspiration. We had been lucky. A moment's hesitation and we could have stopped a fatal cannon shell.

That night, after stand-to, Mac and I were enjoying a fry up in our cramped quarters, when an enemy shell exploded about a hundred yards away in the rear where the lorries were parked. This took us unawares. It was dark with no moon so we extinguished our lamp and listened, counting the seconds between the report of the guns firing and the shells arriving. The dull thuds were from a great distance, the whine of the shells traveling through the air and the resultant explosions kept us below ground. It soon became obvious that the enemy was using several guns.

Our gunners exchanged shell for shell. Enemy shells found their targets but our shells were dispatched to various parts of the valley in the general direction of the enemy gun flashes, without much hope of contact. Our gunners were firing blind to relieve their exasperation. The deafening noise of exploding shells, the squeals of shells in transit, the concussion and the almost continuous whine, as if bodies were suffering torment of being torn asunder, confused us and we had no feeling. We sat and waited whilst the earth shook. Brilliant flashes illuminated everything and the stink of cordite was suffocating. During the pandemonium, there was a deafening explosion, followed by a huge ball of fire that lit up the jungle for miles around.

An enemy shell had exploded in the ammunition pit a few yards away from our foxhole. A sheet of flame, several hundred feet high, rose into the night sky and there was a deafening roar, as the charges ignited. Had we remained in our foxhole Mac and I would certainly have been baked alive. The heat was unbearable as we scrambled out to find a safer place. At the same time, three screaming men, their clothing ablaze, dashed past us and without hesitation, we gave chase and rolled them in the dust to put out the flames. All three were whimpering and suffered shock as we got them down to the command post. We quickly cut away their clothing, smothered them with anti-burn cream and wrapped them in blankets. At first I thought they were three of our own chaps as, in the light of the hurricane lamps, there appeared to be a predominance of white skin, but we soon discovered they were three of our followers. They were all so badly burned, the flesh wept where the skin was missing which necessitated bandages. They had been asleep on top of the ammunition. We never found any trace of the two missing followers who were cremated. The mass of cordite continued to burn for most of the night. There was nothing we could do about it, whilst we remained in the comparative safety of the command post. All that night a ferocious battle was fought further south and ours was not the only fires that burned.

Our casualties during the bombardment were comparatively light. One man vanished when a shell buried itself in the trench in which he sheltered. The only evidence of his existence were a few pieces of flesh and clothing left behind. Several men had minor wounds and some were evacuated with the followers. It was frightening to know that in a fraction of a second we could cease to exist and be spread all over the jungle. We do tend to build up a protective mechanism around ourselves as we prayed during the shelling. The faith that we will survive, enabled us to dismiss all thoughts of death, it's the other chap who would cop it. Some months later we heard that two of the followers had survived their burns and lived.

At first light, enemy shells began to arrive again. The first shell landed amongst our vehicles parked about 200 yards in the rear and minutes later, another shell landed 100 yards in front, then another hit one of our guns, it was apparent that the enemy had established an O.P. somewhere in the surrounding hills at the rear of us. There was no other explanation for the accuracy of their shelling. At intervals that morning, shells continued to fall on our gun site and our gunners returned the fire. The chances of hitting the enemy were remote. In the middle of all this and with laughable intonations, a Dakota transport plane made several runs over the brigade area and dropped supplies, some with, some without parachutes. The shelling ceased about midday as if it was time for lunch and, as nothing happened for more than an hour, men came up out of their foxholes to assess the damage. Two of our guns were write-offs and five lorries were burned out, all laden with stores. During the twenty four hours since the shelling started we had lost twenty six men killed and wounded, including one man who was killed during the airdrop, when a case of corned beef fell squarely on him as he crouched in his slit trench.

Later, a messenger from brigade H.Q. brought the mail and instructions to move back into the hills before dark. Tom handed me a bundle of letters addressed to those no longer with us. I had several letters from home but there was no time to look at them as we feverishly prepared for the move. I hated war and everyone concerned with it and longed to get away from it all.

The adjutant handed me a letter from the army audit department in New Delhi, demanding an explanation as to why, when stationed in Quetta, we used about a hundred thousand pounds weight of coal too much, as the authority we obtained didn't have the authority to issue an authority. He said he would like to see me about it when I had time. As it turned out, I never had the time either and some weeks later, when I remembered it, I couldn't find the letter. It's incredible that, in the middle of a bloody battle the paper war was still in progress. Remember, India was not at war and never would be. What the hell were we doing here?

My jeep, with the trailer overloaded and Mac as passenger, was the leading vehicle on the journey north. We went across country and slowly motored up the steep Chocolate Hill, and before dark, had disappeared into the surrounding hills. Meanwhile the military colossus on both sides continued to consume men who relentlessly pursued each other to kill and to occupy a piece of land on the earth which would never belong to them unless, of course they happened to occupy a small part of it in death, which seemed to be the whole purpose of the exercise. It was hard to understand all the carnage. We were thankful for the respite from further bombardment and prayed for a few days of peace and quiet. The noise from the gunfire and bombardment had affected our hearing and Mac and I found ourselves shouting at each other, even though we had only the noise of the jeep's engine to contend with. Most of our men seemed to be affected similarly. The emotional experience and the effect of the resultant casualties had implanted a new sense of comradeship amongst us.

Although progress was slow, we negotiated Chocolate Hill, following another convoy. We could see the track winding its way northwards out of the battle zone, but we hadn't gone far when everything came to a standstill. Vehicles were lined up nose to tail, the length of the visible track. Progress had been slow, it was move, halt, move, halt, all that day. When evening approached and we had been at the same spot for more than an hour, I sent Mac up ahead on foot to see what was causing the hold up. Despite the twists and turns of the steep track the same hills had been kept in view all day. We were at a sharp bend in the track and there wasn't room for another vehicle to pass. Here, on the offside, the ground disappeared in a precipitous drop of several hundred feet into the valley below, whilst on the nearside, the hill rose almost perpendicular to an immeasurable height.

As twilight approached it became cooler, in fact a chill breeze descended from above. One by one, as the convoys came to a halt, the noise of engines was extinguished and there was complete silence. Walking to the next corner, and in the twilight, I could just see the track, choked with traffic, snaking into the hills and, as it was obvious we would be here for some time, I put the billy on and made tea. Sitting on the sandy track with my back supported by a wheel of the jeep drinking tea, chewing a hard army biscuit, which was all I could find without unloading the truck, I smoked a cigarette.

Earlier on, two Bren gun carriers, full of infantry, had squeezed past the convoy and disappeared up front at speed. Now, nothing moved. Sitting there on my own, I thought I heard someone tell someone else to piss off, and another expressed his doubts about digging up the fucking road, then, above it all, I heard Tom's voice and I knew he was coming to see me. When he arrived he said.

"You're a cunning sod Q, every time I see you, you're drinking tea, any left?"

"Sure." I said, "Help yourself." And I handed him Mac's mug.

"What's happening up front?"

"Mac went to find out ages ago, expect he'll be back soon."

"Mind if I wait a bit? Let's sit down, I've had a hell of a fucking day."

"We all have, let's hope we have a few quiet nights when we're settled again."

"Did you get any mail this morning?"

"Yes, did you?"

"Mmm, but I haven't had a chance to read it yet."

"But that's a pleasure to come. It's too dark now."

Mac was sauntering around the corner, hands in his pockets as if he hadn't a care in the world.

"Where the fucking hell have you been?" said Tom.

"What?"

"You know fucking well what I mean, what's going on up front?"

"Oh. They're trying to clear a Jap roadblock about a mile down the track, apparently a couple of drivers got knocked off this afternoon and their lorries are blocking the road. The Japs have some bunkers up the hill above the road and our infantry have already lost some men trying to get them out."

I sat down on the road, leaned against the cliff at the roadside and lit another cigarette. Tom did the same.

"What a fucking balls up," whispered Tom, "bye-the-way Q, did I see you talking to the engineers officer before we left the old gun site?"

"Yes, he said he was going to fix some more thunder flashes but what I really wanted him for was the destruction of those Studebakers we had to leave behind. Pity that, I would have liked to have kept them, but we haven't enough drivers, he said he would try to use them, but if not, would make sure no one else does."

"Bye-the-way Mac." said Tom. "You're a bloody fool wandering about without a fucking rifle, don't do it again, you should know better than that."

"Don't you want to hear the rest of the story?" Mac asked.

"All right then, let's have it, only don't fuck about, I should start getting back."

"I went up to within two hundred yards of the road block." Mac said. "I was chatting to some of the infantry blokes, when there was a hell of a fucking bang, shit flying everywhere and they reckoned it was the Japs who had rolled a large grenade down the hill. The thing is, they don't know how many Japs there are up there. But one thing's certain, we are here for the rest of the night, at least."

"Ah well, there's nothing we can do. We can't get a gun through this lot unless we tip a few vehicles over the side and I can't see that happening."

"Is that what took you so long?" I asked.

"No, matter of fact Q, there's a signals truck down there and they were listening to the radio news from London, so I listened with then. They confirmed Imphal was cut off from both ends and there's a hell of a fucking battle going on at Kohima. They seem to know more about the bloody war out here than we do. They said something about a British Second Division coming to the rescue but there was a lot of static and I couldn't hear very well. They say the British Second is an armored Division."

"Look, I can't stay any longer, hope no one takes a fucking pot shot at me and hope to see you in the morning, cheers." Tom went back to the guns.

It was very dark that night with no moon and no one bothered about a black-out as cigarettes were lit all along the track on both sides of us, enough to give us confidence to get some sleep.

It was pleasantly cool during the night and well before the sun was overhead again we were on the move. Our infantry had cleared the road-block, lorries had been pushed over the side, and we were told to keep on the move. At one point we were stopped by infantry who told us not to hang about for the next few hundred yards as there were still some Japs about, so we broke all speed records for the next half-mile. The track ascended for the next few miles until we were about a thousand feet up and all the hills were larger and almost perpendicular. The track, cut into the hillside in the soft clay, was tricky to negotiate.

The place allocated to us as a gun site was almost at the summit. The hill was steep with a deep plunge into the jungle of over a thousand feet. As far as the eye could see, the yellow track snaked away into the distance, but we were on a natural platform just about large enough to accommodate our guns side by side. There was no cover but we didn't think we would ever need it up here. In front and to our right was a deep chasm as the valley fell away and the bottom was concealed in a deep blue mist. As a backdrop to the site, a small hillock was useful in which to dig our foxholes. Nearly all our vehicles were parked wheel to wheel, on the blind side of this hillock, just off the track, at a point where it was wider. We buried our ammunition in the hillside. Looking east, the range of hills stretched unbroken in similar contour to the hills on our side of the valley. However our troops occupied the largest hills that dominated the surrounding countryside. To our rear and opposite the parked vehicles and the main track the ground dropped and could easily be defended.

There was a similar range of hills, a few hundred yards distant. To the front and on our left, three large hills stood out and as these dominated the track, this position was to be held at all costs. We had at least three months to wait for the monsoons. Up here we felt free from enemy infantry, the sky was clear and blue, the air clean and cool, but we still concentrated on our digging.

As best I could, I dug a miniature cave in the side of the hillock but the earth was stony and wouldn't hold. Eventually my foxhole resembled a rabbit hole into which I squeezed myself, feet first. Nothing appeared to move on the hills between the enemy and us. But as all the hills were thickly wooded and covered by dense undergrowth this was not surprising. We knew that several infantry companies were digging in near us but we couldn't see them either. Our little hill eventually resembled a rabbit warren with many half-dug holes abandoned. With pick and entrenching tools, all digging was soon completed and the men rested.

A mile along the track, and to our rear, was a temporary field hospital. Here was a small plateau on which tents had been erected. Nearby was a pumping station, with a pipe descending into the valley and water was collected from this point. Gurkha occupied the next hill to us, and every time the water truck appeared they came down to fill their water bottles. We were always happy to see them.

Looking through our field glasses one morning we noticed the undergrowth had been cleared near the summit of the hill opposite and there, fully exposed to view, were the Japs building bunkers.

There seemed rather a lot of them and we had to presume they could see us, as we were very exposed. There was now a feeling of foreboding and frustration as we waited for them to take the initiative again. A sense of urgency prevailed. The situation of their bunkers was well outside the range of small arms fire. A few days later, after abortive attempts by our infantry to dislodge them from their bunkers had failed, our gun with the shortened barrel was sent forward. We watched through binoculars as our gunners, situated on the track opposite the bunkers, fired over open sights at point blank range. It seemed as if, when one bunker was knocked out another was discovered and they seemed to spread like an infectious disease. Some time after our gun had returned, the five remaining guns supported an infantry attack, but as fast as one Jap was put out of action two more took his place.

We had by now, established an O.P. on the largest hill named Gibraltar. Here we had an officer and two signalers and they were with a Scottish battalion. I sent hot meals up to them in vacuum flasks whilst it was quiet. Several times our guns were called on for supporting fire, but the action was mostly at night.

Early one morning, just after sunrise, we were taken by surprise by a Jap whiz-bang. We called it a whiz-bang for want of a better name, as that's the only warning we got, a whiz-bang. The shell arrived and exploded at almost the same time as we heard the sound of the gun being fired. There was no warning and no defense for our exposed position. It appeared the guns were being fired from bunkers newly dug on the hill where similar bunkers had recently been destroyed. In view of the fact that we had only one second to take cover, and the shells kept coming in a haphazard manner most of the day, any movement above ground was at high speed. I wished my foxhole were deeper, as did many others. It was soon obvious the enemy had an O.P. in the bunkers opposite us.

Late one afternoon there was the thump of a large gun being fired from some distance to the south, followed by the whine of the shell in transit and the shattering explosion as the projectile hit the earth. The first shell dropped short of our position in the valley below and no damage was done, the second shell however, was nearer and after it had screamed past overhead, it exploded in the rear of our position, near enough to cause concern. This was a Jap 150 mm howitzer. Our own guns were now brought into action.

First one gun fired then others with corrections. Another shell whizzed overhead. I laid on my stomach in my small cave and watched the action. I saw the flash of the Jap mountain gun, if that's what it was, counted the seconds between the thuds and the explosions of the larger guns and expected to be blown to pieces at any moment.

All our guns fired at the same time and whiz-bangs arrived and exploded amongst the guns causing casualties and then as a complete surprise, a 25-pounder regiment dug in on a hill behind us dispatched several salvos in quick succession into the hill opposite, silencing the whiz-bangs for the time being. In the pandemonium, the screams of many shells passing overhead with those newly arriving, the concussion from our own guns and the unexpected explosions near at hand was very disconcerting and enough to put the strongest mind off balance. I was sorry for those who suffered from dysentery, as in these circumstances; a bowel action is uncontrollable. Every time the ground shook with a deafening explosion, I found myself curled in a fetus position, rolling up as small as possible, to convince myself that I will be safe and that it's the other chaps who will cop it. Those who boast they have no fear are either liars or already dead. I think I must have been a bit scared, as in the fog of dust and the overwhelming stench of cordite, I just couldn't breath, but I continued to lie there and to listen. I didn't know what else to do. Later, an enemy shell must have landed on top of the little hillock as the earth fell on me and I was buried in dirt and stones. I dug myself upwards out of my premature grave and eventually I could see the sky. Then suddenly, quietness reigned as if someone had pulled a switch.

One by one we came up out of our foxholes and gave what assistance we could to the casualties whom we got away to the field hospital. Tea was brewed in a dozen places.

The enemy gave us time to clear up the mess and waited until after dark to take advantage of us again. Then distant thuds heralded further shelling.

My mind was now muddled and whilst I was trying to decide whether or not to leave my foxhole and where else to go, two heavy shells arrived simultaneously. One was a direct hit on one of our guns and another fell to the rear of the little hillock causing a sheet of fire to light up the surrounding hills. It was now dark and flames leapt skywards as our stock of ammunition, buried in the hillside began to explode in the heat. It was too hot for me to stay any longer or I would be roasted alive, so I made my way down to the lower slope in the hope of finding shelter. I crawled out and down and had a quick look to see whether anything could be done to douse the fires but recognized there was now more than one lorry alight. Another lorry laden with several forty gallon barrels of petrol looked as if would catch fire at any moment. No one could possibly approach from the road level whilst the ammunition continued to explode.

I slithered down, pressing my head between my hands into the ground every time another shell exploded and wished I could disappear underground when I bumped into Mac. He was of the same mind and we met head on half way down the hill. Our stock of shells were now exploding on the far side of the hillock and shrapnel screamed in all directions. One after another, our lorries caught fire and added to the noise and illuminations. Two more enemy shells landed nearby, covering us with earth and stones and we finished our journey on all fours, monkey fashion and found a hole where other gunners were sheltering. They made room for us. Five of us crouched in this little trench and we all lit cigarettes whilst the fires illuminated everything for all to see for miles around. There were no more whiz-bangs that night but larger shells continued to arrive as we made a good target. The enemy was content to send a shell in our direction at infrequent intervals, to keep the fires burning. Our ammunition continued to explode and one after another the vehicles burned themselves out.

At daybreak, the shelling ceased and we watched a huge column of smoke from the fires ascending straight into the clear blue sky. There was no wind. No doubt this must have given pleasure to the Japs, as this could be seen many miles distant.

I emptied the jeep and trailer and helped get the wounded to the field hospital. The men were strapped on to stretches and secured to the vehicles. I met Tom with our new officer and we decided to let the fires burn themselves out. There was nothing we could do whilst shells continued to explode.

The gun site was in a mess. One gun had disappeared over the side of the hill into the valley below and couldn't be seen. Of the three guns overturned, one was a write-off. All the gun's wheel tires were punctured. During the night we had lost two guns, and an unknown number of lorries and nineteen men killed, one missing and several wounded. What a bloody waste.

When I was down at the hospital, I learned the R.A.F. were in process of flying the 5th Indian Division into Imphal from the Arakan front and these troops were being used to get the roads open from both sides, especially the road back to Kohima. There were still roadblocks directly behind, that cut us off from Imphal.

Tom was waiting for me when I arrived back at the gun site.

"Thank goodness you're back Q. We can't stop here any longer; orders are to quit as soon as possible after sunset. The adjutant has already left to reconnoiter a site on the other side of the field hospital and he's left me in charge until we can do something with this new bloke."

"What about bringing the other chap down from the O.P.?"

"Afraid he bought it last night, and the two signalers with him."

"That's tough, they had a number eleven set up there and a charging plant not to mention a field telephone and other equipment. We're getting desperately short of equipment you know."

"Look Q, leave it to me, the adjutant will go up to the O.P. just as soon as we've settled in the new position, then I'll see if the new bloke can take over."

"What's he like Tom?"

"Bloody useless, too young! Want's a fucking nurse maid."

We walked down towards the blackened chassis of the burnt out lorries. The heat had exploded all our ammunition and the hill had collapsed, burying what remained. The chassis were a mangled heap of unrecognizable iron. Even the water wagon was now useless, full of big holes. Eleven lorries were burned out, with the remains of their engines where they had fallen.

"We're in the shit now Tom, no water."

"We'll have to scrounge from one of the other units, don't worry Q, the Adjutant has already sent a sitrep off to brigade. I don't suppose we'll get replacements out, but at least they know the position."

"Remember my tin trunk, the one I bought in Quetta? There it is, that jagged piece of metal. I had lots of things stored there, things ready to take home for my kids, there was a pair of Jap binoculars, caps and lots of swords and several other bits and pieces I'd been asked to take care of. Various officers had handed things to me for safe keeping such as pens, watches, photographs and all the personal things from the chaps that have been killed, things we were hoping to send to their next of kin."

I was thankful our reserves of rations had been distributed over all the remaining lorries and that I had Mac to look after things. Soon after sunset the three guns were winched up on to the track and towed away to the new gun site. The gun with the shortened barrel had already left. We followed.

We were glad to get away from this place, known as Shenam Saddle, and I shall never forget it, it was the most disastrous three weeks of my life, so far.

EIGHTEEN

W E DIDN'T KNOW it at the time, but this was to be our last resting place and our next move would be back to civilization. But not for another five months and a lot would happen before then.

The new site was spacious with a gentle slope rising from the track for about two hundred yards, then a sudden rise to the summit that was out of sight, but it appeared to be about three hundred feet to the top. Opposite, on the other side of the track, the ground fell away for several hundred feet with a wide valley below and further hills in the distance. Short stumpy trees gave us shelter from the sun and the undergrowth was not so prolific. The place was called Tengoupal, although no one knew why. The hills and jungle had a prehistoric appearance even though the narrow jeep track, which was the main thoroughfare, looked as if it had been recently constructed for this war. A short time ago it was a mule track. We didn't know it then, but on top of the hill behind us, was a section of an Indian Mountain Regiment, they were Sikhs and were equipped with small mountain guns and three-inch mortars. Also, we hoped for our protection, and only a few hundred yards away down the track, was a company of Gurkhas.

The three guns were dug in near the track and the sawn off gun kept mobile. All the remaining vehicles were parked as far away from the track as possible, taking advantage of the jungle cover.

We dug long slit trenches and constructed covered Bren gun posts, introducing the system of signaling by means of old telephone wires, tied round our wrists or ankles, in order to maintain silence during the hours of darkness. Jungle growth was cleared, barbed wire and booby traps fixed all round the perimeter. When all this was done, we waited and listened. By courtesy of an Indian Battalion, a water wagon called on us every day and water was rationed for drinking purposes only. But the lads were not slow in asking at every opportunity to take advantage of the situation. Despite the loss of so many supplies, ammunition and rations were sufficient for the time being.

Before going forward to the O.P. on Gibraltar, which we could still see from the new site, I met our adjutant. I had the greatest respect for him from the first meeting in Hitchin, and we had built up a close rapport. Now he handed me his watch, fountain pen, wallet and personal papers, said goodbye and told me he wouldn't be back as he was convinced the Japs were about to make a big push forward. Mac and I joked with him and couldn't believe anything would happen to him, he was such a decent chap. It had been quiet for a few days, the sun was shining from a clear blue sky, and we hadn't had any news from anywhere to worry us.

A massive frontal attack was expected at any moment. The enemy would be compelled to take desperate measures to improve their position before the monsoon rains, if they were to survive. But the rains were not expected for another eight weeks or more. It was only mid-April and normally, the monsoons would not be expected until the end of June.

Using a large gun, the enemy dropped shells down in the valley opposite, whether intended for us or overshooting the larger hills, we did not know. We watched the flash of the explosion as the shells landed and all was silent as we witnessed the destructive effect. Shrapnel expanded in an ever-increasing circle felling trees and branches in its path. Then we heard the report of the explosion, followed by the whine of the shell in the air, all in reverse order. The noise was magnified and echoed many times as concussions reverberated across the valley.

I was able to detach myself from the battles further south and slept at night in my foxhole, with the telephone wires fixed to my ankles and wrists, in the knowledge that someone was on guard duty and I would not be killed in my sleep.

A few days after we had settled in, the main attack began.

Previously our gunners had registered targets and during the night were called upon to fire. They were busy for the remainder of that night. The 25-pounders joined the melee and the hillside was lit by many Very lights. In the thunder of a thousand small arms and mortar fire, the enemy was driven off with heavy losses. If the Japs took the forward hills now occupied by us, there was nothing to stop them occupying Imphal, then India. Everyone, including all the men who were ill with dysentery or diarrhea and walked around with holes in their underwear, if they had any, were called to fight.

I was sitting in my trench with the wires connected to my hand and feet. I had a Bren gun now, set up so I could spray as many bullets as I could towards the barbed wire, without poking my head over the top. I had as many grenades as I could collect. On either side of me were two-man Bren guns with fields of fire set up to protect our remaining gun emplacements. We knew the Japs would try to storm the guns and blow them up, even if they were killed doing it. At the far end of their supply line, they were desperate. The Japs had no food, little ammo but their bayonets and swords and their courage. We did not recognize it as such back then, we saw them as just fanatical. Without the rum I did not have such courage. I just wanted to get it over with. I had so much to live for but was sick of all the carnage and the senseless waste of life around us. I was homesick and determined to get back alive and see my children.

That first night was more intense than Chocolate Hill or the battles we fought at Shenam Saddle. Waves of Japs stormed us. They seemed to come from everywhere and did not stop charging and screaming their battle cries. My Bren gun barrel should have melted that night. I had preloaded as many magazines as I could and used them all. Between magazine changes I threw a grenade, or two. As dawn broke I took a chance to peak over the side of my trench. There was no response to my tugs on either side of me and the guns were silent. All I could hear were flies, millions of them. I had one grenade left and I held it at the ready as I looked out over a mass of dead Japanese. There was one officer, or part of him almost at the top of my trench. His eyes stared at me. I dropped the grenade, thankful I had not pulled the pin and went in search, on my hands and knees, through our trenches, to see if any soldiers were still alive. Replacements came to the gun positions around me and I was glad to see them sorting out the dead and preparing their guns for the next wave of suicide charges. I wanted to get a cup of tea and see who was still alive that I knew. I never found out the names of the dead gunners near me.

Later in the morning the battle started up again. I was in a new trench with my Bren and more grenades. I still had my Sten gun but only a couple of magazines. We had everyone armed and ready to fight, as we did not know where the Japs would attack next. We lost touch with our O.P. as wave after wave of the enemy stormed the hills. The Gurkhas and several other small companies left their positions nearby and marched forward as reinforcements. I always felt safer with Gurkhas around. They are the ultimate fighters. On the parade ground they would draw their kukris and once unsheathed they would have to cover them in blood. There was always a poor goat tied to a stake at the end of the parade ground. They made short work of the goat as they did any Jap they came across.

It was not until the morning of the third day that we were exhausted and could fight no longer. Hills had changed hands several times and there was great loss of life. The remnants of the Burma Japanese Army slunk back into the jungle. We had defeated the Imperial Japanese Army, their first ever defeat.

This was the most crucial battle of the Burma campaign and the bloodiest. Later that day, we learned the road to Palel had been opened and a convoy of ambulances passed our lines. Although grateful the wounded would be cared for, our greatest hope was that we would soon receive some decent rations. I heard that a Japanese officer had been taken prisoner and was in one of the ambulances on his way to Imphal. As I watched the convoy, Gurkhas came down from the hill opposite, stopped the convoy, took the prisoner and walked up the hill with him. They all had their kukris drawn and I could only guess what happened to him.

Infantry reinforcements now marched forward in small companies. I saw Gurkhas, who, under their slouch hats, didn't look more than fourteen years old. I hadn't been back from Palel after collecting supplies, when Tom came to see me and told me the news that our adjutant and the two signalers were missing. He wanted me to go with him up to the O.P. to search for them. There weren't enough hours of daylight left so we decided to go first thing next morning. The only officer we had now was the young second lieutenant whom I shall refer to as Lieutenant Short and he was sick with dysentery so we left him in charge, for what use that was. We took two gunners with us to the forward hill, parked the jeep where instructed by the military police and walked up the hill to where our O.P was supposed to be located. A blackened mass of tree stumps replaced what, a few days earlier, had been a lush forest. Infantry were in the process of clearing the carnage of three days of battle. The aftermath of the slaughter was gruesome. Decomposing human remains and clothing littered the area covered in millions of flies.

We found the three bodies of our men and added our vomit, then hurried away. Bodies, hundreds of then, ours and the enemy, were being heaved down on to the track where they were bulldozed way down to the lower slopes, to be buried at some future time. The track was thick in congealed slime and blood and alive with maggots as they fought to devour the bodies. Some bodies were already bloated and the stench of death lingered with me for days. As the clearing up troops performed their task, there was an occasional pistol shot. I hurried away, nausea overtaking me. I glimpsed the huge mounds of bodies that numbered several thousand. It was hard to estimate numbers in that massacre.

The two opposing bodies of men had successfully disposed of each other in accordance with military tradition. The Japanese obsession to commit harakiri and join their ancestors with all speed was a major failing in their military strategy. Their losses were at least ten to our one.

When we arrived back at the gun sight we learned that Jap roadblocks had again cut the road back to Palel. This time it was more serious when they attacked the airstrip at Palel and destroyed several planes on the ground. They now occupied the hills surrounding the airstrip.

To relieve the monotony I began to ration out the rum. It worked out that twenty men shared a pint mug of neat rum and they drank this before evening stand-to. After stand-to each evening, Tom, Mac and I got into the habit of having an extra tot before we settled in for the night. Sometimes it was more than one.

One morning I awoke rather late and remembered we had more than our fair share of rum the previous evening. I lay for some time waiting and listening before I roused myself. I could not remember getting onto my bed in my foxhole and there hadn't been any excitement during the night as the wire was still tied to my ankle. Mac was always so punctual with the morning tea and I suspected he had also overslept. So I laced up my boots and went along to the nearest Bren gun post to see whether anything had occurred during the night.

They had had morning stand-to and breakfast; such as it was, so I went to see what had happened to Mac. I was surprised when I found him still on his blanket and gave him a shake. He did not respond, so I pulled him feet first into the open. I just couldn't believe he was dead. I am sure he had only just died, as he was still warm. I called for assistance and we took him down to the field hospital, but they could do nothing. Later, we learned he had died of malarial meningitis that until then, we had known as scrub typhus. Many of our men died in this manner. Mac had always been fit and strong and he had been so full of fun the previous evening.

Tom insisted that, as we were now so short of men, every man should have someone to take over, should it be necessary, and he suggested sergeant Bill Lowe. So Bill moved into the stores dump, such as it was. He had been in charge of the sawn off gun, which had recently seen action. He took charge of the rum but argued it would never match whiskey. He now tapped the barrel, as our stock of bottled rum was nearly exhausted. The liquid from the barrel was thick and black and was very potent, so it had to be taken in small doses. Half a pint of it put me to sleep very quickly, and one night I passed out on the short journey from the tarpaulin covered stores dug out to my foxhole. It was only a matter of a few yards but I slept out in the open all night where I had fallen and didn't remember how I got there.

I must tell you of the incident of the missing contents of a bottle of rum of which I was reminded in an unexpected manner some twenty-five years later. As was my habit, since Mac died, before evening stand-to, I took a walk down the hill and had a word with the gunners. It got pretty lonely being a senior N.C.O. and with not much to do. As a point of discipline, I always wore my webbing equipment, a steel helmet and my Sten gun on stand-to. To save time, should anyone be sick enough to require rum to be administered to them, I kept my water bottle full of rum and had an occasional swig during stand-to. The incident concerned second lieutenant Short who was very sick with dysentery. I felt sorry for him. He was much too young to be out here in Burma. He must have come to us straight from the boat as he brought with him all his officers kit, as prescribed by peacetime regulations. He had lots of camping gear such as camp bed, camp bath, washbasin and a small tent and many other things considered necessary. How all the kit went missing was a mystery.

Within a few days of joining us he was out of action from dysentery. I hadn't had anything to do with him until the day he sent word he wanted to see me. I found him trying to dig himself a hole in which to sleep and as he was obviously very sick, I got some of the lads to help. They found and erected his tent. I couldn't persuade him to go to the field hospital for treatment and it was hopeless to try to clean him up as he was in a filthy state. But I managed to get him down in his tent and on his blanket. Reluctantly, I agreed to let him have one of the precious bottles of rum he asked for, poured him a good measure, which he swallowed and left the bottle with him.

So far as I knew, no one went near him until Tom arrived back from the O.P. where he had been for a couple of days, and by this time he was in such a state we had to get him down to the hospital.

That was the last we saw of him. I collected the remainder of his kit and the bottle of rum and put everything into stores. That evening, after stand-to Tom suggested we finish the remains of that bottle of rum, so, sitting under the stores tarpaulin we proceeded to share it out.

Tom was first to take a mouthful that he immediately spat out.

"Jesus Christ! Piss! You taste."

Someone had drunk the rum and urinated in the bottle. We were sickened by this and wondered who could have played such a trick. Had we known, we would have inflicted injury on the culprit.

Half way up the hill, I heard a cockney voice shout, "Hi Q! Who pissed in the officer's rum?"

We spent most of our time resting now. There was nothing to relieve the monotony. Our diet was foul and we talked of deserting as the war looked as if it was going on forever. Bill, who had a sense of humor, talked of his life in India and the Jute mills, the generosity of his employers who had never seen the mills, and of his adventures during his twenty-five years there. He was older, a bachelor and pretty wealthy and extracted a promise from me that if we were lucky to get out of this place alive, I would spend at least a month at his house in Calcutta, whether we were granted leave or not.

The situation wasn't very promising. Most of our men had something wrong with them, dysentery, jungle sores or a touch of malaria through not taking mepacrine tablets. We were cut off from Palel and the outside world. We couldn't get supplies and some miles further back, the Japs still battled at Kohima. Yet on our front the war had come to a standstill, or so it seemed.

However, at about ten o'clock that night, I was trying to get comfortable in my foxhole. I had just finished my nightcap and fixed the wire to my ankle, when the wire became taut. The gunner at the other end was pulling and jerking vigorously, I guessed something was amiss. I quickly put on my boots, collected my kit, Sten gun and pouches and crawled to my place in the slit trench, picked up the other wire which I placed around my wrist, gave it a sharp tug which was acknowledged, and sat down on an empty ammunition box to wait. I had given the Bren back to a new two-man team and felt comfortable with my Sten gun, as long as I had enough grenades. I had found some more magazines and ammunition.

The rum had made me drowsy and I didn't feel like waiting around. It was a beautiful night with no moon and very quiet. I sat there for what seemed like an hour, nodding and fighting against sleep, not hearing anything and wondering whether I was the only one left alive in the world. Fed up, I made my way slowly along the trench to the covered Bren gun pit, where there were two men on duty. I surprised them. I hadn't made any noise. I wanted to know what prompted the stand-to. Apparently, a Jap patrol had been seen boldly walking along the main track and all the units in the vicinity had been alerted.

I asked them to give my wire a tug when it was time to stand-down and made my way back to my ammunition box. Field telephones connected each Bren gun pit with our Command Post, which, in turn, had direct communication with Brigade H.Q.; so all the units around us were only a phone call away.

Sitting there, dozing, with a dry mouth and a tongue like the bottom of a birdcage, I tried to keep awake when I distinctly heard a rustle in the undergrowth, just outside our perimeter wire. As I listened, I heard the rattle of stones in an empty can fixed to the wire, then the snip, which sounded like wire being cut, so I gave my wire a tug and this was acknowledged. I was wide-awake now and my heart was racing, I was certain all the activity was on the wire about thirty feet away from me. Our new drill was to explode three or more grenades in quick succession as a signal to the Indian mountain gun company higher up the hill behind us, who would then put down mortar fire around our perimeter, previously registered as targets at the same time. The Gurkhas on the next hill would fire Very pistols to give us light, and we would do the same for them.

Then the invaders abandoned all precautions, there was much noise and this confirmed their presence so the two men in the Bren gun post nearest me each lobbed over three grenades and I did likewise.

Suddenly, in my fuddled state, I had pulled the pins and thrown a dozen grenades I had in a box by my side. Mortar shells exploded lower down the hill and clods of earth flew in all directions. Very lights burst and hung in the sky above us, lighting the jungle as brilliantly as daylight. I found some more grenades and threw them over for good measure. The raiding party was cut down by crossfire from our Bren guns and I couldn't imagine anyone being left alive after all that. Plucking up courage to look over the top of the trench, I saw what looked like several bodies crawling up the slope towards me. This shocked me as they were so near. In the excitement, I emptied two magazines of ammunition into them from my Sten gun. Meantime the Bren guns continued to fire bursts into the bodies and the Jungle beyond. Mortar bombs continued to explode down the hill and more Very lights hung in the sky. The dry undergrowth was now alight in many places.

When the Bren gunners ceased firing, I made my way towards them and we looked down towards the perimeter wire where it was clear that nothing moved. I phoned Tom in the command post and he must have informed the other units, as suddenly all was quiet. The whole action took only about three minutes and we had no casualties. Several fires burned all night but were not serious and gave us light, but we didn't leave the trench until daylight. The stench of cordite, smoke from the fires and other smells was nothing compared to the fog of our cigarette smoke as we puffed away, thankful to be alive.

At daybreak Tom and I climbed out of the trench whilst the Bren gunners kept us covered. The dead Japs looked as if they had suffered from malnutrition. They were very small in stature. With care we inspected them, mindful of the fact they often booby trapped their own bodies, but they looked harmless enough so we left them and gave instructions to the Bren gunners to shoot anything that moved whilst we obtained assistance from the infantry to collect the bodies and their firearms.

Twenty-three bodies were recovered and taken away, their own peculiar smell with them. Later that day a Gurkha patrol found and ambushed a few Jap stragglers. They must have been part of the same raiding party.

The excitement left us all exhausted. Perimeter wires and booby traps had to be reset and ammunition replaced. Smoke from fires on the surrounding hills; hunger for a good meal and the memory of colleagues now dead left me despondent. Tea was the one thing we always fell back on, but Bill wouldn't make it and I missed Mac. I think most of us suffered from shattered nerves and dysentery.

Our bedraggled appearance didn't help. My body was dirty, my hair unkempt and the long beard made me feel lousy. I could not get enough sleep but had to stay alert, so the slightest noise left me feeling exhausted.

The news that the road was expected to be open soon was welcome. With this in mind I decided to write home to my wife and my parents, in the hope we would be able to get the letters away. I addressed a letter but was stuck. I did not know what to write. What do you say when you haven't received letters for several weeks? I would have to ignore what had happened here as it was bound to be censored. So I lit a cigarette and sat staring into space. Tom joined me.

"Any tea? I'd thought I'd catch up."

"Help yourself."

"Where's Bill?"

"Asleep, lazy sod. Can't get him to make tea."

"Writing home?"

"Trying to. Can't think what to write about. Was enthusiastic a few moments ago but the feeling has left me. Now I'm stumped."

"I did the same thing, just sat there. What can you say that has not been said before? You know Q, I'm getting to the point of believing the old soldiers tale that if you don't see someone for long enough, you not only forget what they look like, but can quite easily forget them altogether. I can understand why some of the regulars went a bit balmy when they hadn't seen their wives for over seven years and were then told they would have to wait a few more years, or until the war is over. What annoys me is that the Aussies and Kiwis only do about eighteen months overseas, then get home leave. Whilst we're left to sweat it out. The bastards back home don't give a fuck about us."

"What about the Yanks then?"

"Those useless pricks! Twelve months is their maximum stint overseas, and then they get a medal. They get medals for almost everything."

"Nice cup of Cha that."

"Haven't seen the water wagon today, hope it comes soon as we are almost out of water. You might enquire if you're going down to the command post, Tom."

"What I came about Q was a couple of the lads think they saw a bull or cow this morning when they went for a walk. It was some distance away but they don't roam far and I thought it might be an idea if we got a party together and went after it. What do you think?"

"Good idea. I'll warn the cooks. We would have to chase it near the track, otherwise we'll never get it here."

After Tom left I finished the letters without further hassle.

That evening Tom, Bill and I debated what to do about the sitrep from IV Corps instructing Tom to supply five names for military decorations. They had given him twenty-four hours to reply. Well, we didn't know whom to suggest. We could easily have put our own names forward, but that wouldn't have been right. So we compiled a list of our evacuated wounded, put the names of all those we could remember into a hat and picked out five. The composition of some of the citations was amusing. We never did manage to catch that animal.

Jap raiding parties were everywhere during the next few days. One vicious attack took place in early afternoon on our position. The humid atmosphere had most of the men relaxing or sleeping in their foxholes but the first explosion instantly had us reaching for boots and helmets. As we crawled out there was another explosion. The bastards destroyed the gun nearest the track with a pole charge and our lads chased them off with grenades and small arms fire. By the time I got anywhere near, the raid was over. The incident took only a couple of minutes. Unfortunately the gun they destroyed was loaded with the shell rammed home and the only way of emptying it would have been to fire it but this would have caused complications as we had been ordered to conserve ammunition. Two of our men were killed. The four wounded, we got away to the field hospital.

On the way back from collecting stores at Palel I noticed a water buffalo in the undergrowth about a mile from our gun site. So next day with Tom's co-operation, a small party of us took one of the Matadors, found the cow, chased it nearer the track and killed it, winched it onto the lorry and brought it back to camp. Traffic was restricted and heavy as convoys passed at certain times in each direction, so we had to follow the convoys, one way or the other. We had only one chap who professed to be a butcher but the promise of a share of fresh meat brought another butcher from a nearby infantry unit. The cow was winched off the lorry and hung by cable in a tree where the butchers got to work. They hadn't been working on the carcass for very long when the Sikhs on the hill above us protested at the slaughter of one of their holy cows and became hostile. We had no intention of relinquishing our prize and moved our Bren gun carrier up, with guns mounted, aimed at their direction. The Indians continued to shout and protest, even after we had erected a tarpaulin. But they quieted down and eventually retired to their own position. This was the first fresh meat we had had for many months and it was greatly overrated but the gesture was appreciated. We had Bombay roast that day and stew was on the boil for the next twenty-four hours, until all the meat was consumed. Fresh vegetables would have helped; we had almost forgotten what they tasted like.

News of battles won at Kohima was most encouraging as the Second Armored Division battled their way towards Imphal and relief was at last in sight.

NINETEEN

T HEN THE RAINS came. As savage as a bombardment, the rain bucketed down. Thunder roared and lightning flashed, as the monsoon took control and the war came to a halt. Sheets of rain and floodwaters swept down the hills. The storm lasted for seventeen days and nights. It filled our trenches and fox holes. Our greatest enemy was now the wet and the cold. We were always saturated. The monsoon effectively halted all movement and flooding washed away the roads.

For the next few weeks we slept on the floors of our vehicles, until the rain eased and we could erect tarpaulins outside. This was a wretched period for us as we were continually soaked to the skin and fires would not burn. Matches and cigarettes had special treatment; even so, it was impossible to light cigarettes, which added to our frustration. Mosquitoes abounded, as did the leaches, and to attend a call of nature was a punishment. During this period several men went down to the field hospital for treatment and another man died in his sleep. There were no new outbreaks of dysentery as many of us were now immune.

News was reassuring as the rains eased and the road from Kohima was at last open. Now the XXXIII Corps began to move south towards us, and every day fresh troops passed our lines.

One morning, an officer, identified as such, even though he was not wearing any insignias, came to our gun site and spoke to the men. It wasn't until after he departed that I discovered no one had challenged him or knew who he was. He asked the men on No.1. gun if they had any complaints, which was a mistake, because I could hear them fucking this and bullocking that. This chap made his way up the hill and spoke to Tom and I. He was well informed and told us we would be relieved soon and be on leave and that our rations would soon improve. Well, that wouldn't be too difficult, we hadn't had much anyway. However, he did promise that, if at all possible, we would each receive a bottle of beer. But this was subject to supplies.

A few days later, I was able to collect one bottle of beer per man for the regiment, so we had more than our share, plus several loaves of fresh bread, the first for nearly a year. Our rations did begin to improve. The contents of each bottle of beer, when opened, shot up into the air and much was lost. Some men were too sick to touch it and we had sufficient to last for several days. Then an accumulation of several months of mail arrived, and so began the harrowing task of separating mail addressed to our dead comrades but bringing joy to those of us left, after so many empty weeks.

As the monsoon rains eased, activity of troop movements and the noise of battle increased, the armies of both sides had reinforced and were ready for battle again. Early one morning, I was awakened by the thunder of dozens of guns pounding enemy hill positions about three miles away. Even at that distance the earth shook from the concussions. The guns and the whine of hundreds of shells and the noise of explosions filled the air and echoed in the hills and valleys. We were at last on the offensive. Through our field glasses we watched Lysander dive-bombers in action, watched the 4.5-inch ack-ack guns and the fast firing Bofas, firing into the hills opposite. We were ignored now and so far as our battery was concerned, the war seemed to be over for us. Many new units and a mass of equipment passed along the track and twice a day I followed the traffic, back and forth, to Palel.

One fine morning we were invaded by military police and top brass in their gold braid. I recognized the leader as the chap who visited us earlier.

He was General Slim. We had no idea who he was on the first visit. This time there were no complaints. He spoke to the men and told us that, as soon as 2nd Division had passed through, we would go back to Imphal and would all get leave. He told us how proud he was of his troops.

That evening Bill and I were celebrating when two R.A.F. chaps casually walked up to our trenches. They wandered up to where I was sitting as if they hadn't a care in the world. Three days earlier we had watched a Lysander go down in flames behind enemy lines. The dive-bomber crashed in the jungle and we thought the two-man crew were dead. They had been trying to find their way back to our lines and were lucky to have found us. They were the same chaps who had visited our mess at Quetta, nearly three years previously, our contact for the whiskey supplies. We gave them a meal and plenty to drink.

They were New Zealanders who were in London at the start of the war and had volunteered for the R.A.F. They had done a lot of flying in other parts of the world. During the two days they were with us, I learned something about New Zealand and hoped one day to go there. Back at the mess we continued the celebrations. I drove them to their R.A.F. base at Palel, after they had drunk all our rum.

Strange troops and unfamiliar uniforms appeared from time to time. Tall black men from the East African Divisions put us to shame with their speech and Oxford accents. It seemed the whole British Empire was on the march south.

When we arrived back at the gun site we were met by a group of men sent as reinforcements including three new officers. We had to trim our hair and shave. During the monsoon period we hadn't bothered about stand-to but this practice was now reinstated. This was a happy time with leave in the offing and we didn't mind some discipline.

It was late October 1944 when, the monsoon over and the sun hotter than ever, the unit received orders to move back to Imphal. The evening before the move, we consumed all the liquor, and during the celebration, dumped everything we didn't need. There was a great deal of merriment and cat calling as we passed other units, almost a carnival all the way into Imphal. A welcoming party escorted us to a canteen and we had a hot meal, whilst beds were provided under new tentage. Next morning after the bliss of a hot bath, new clean uniforms, and a final hair trim and a full stomach, we were impatient to get moving. They wanted us out of the way as quickly as possible.

Surprisingly, we were given the choice of leave to anywhere in India. Some decided to go as far away as possible, but Tom, Bill, and I decided on Calcutta. Bill insisted we spend time with him at his bungalow before reporting to the leave centre. Our leave passes stated that leave would commence on the day we reported at our destination, as stated on the leave pass, which was The Sergeants Leave Centre, Museum Buildings, Chowringhee, Calcutta. We now looked forward to all those comforts we had missed out on; a clean toilet, instead of squatting over a hole in the ground and being bitten by hundreds of flies in the process, to lay on a soft mattress with clean sheets, to wash and shave in hot water and to soak in a hot bath, and to eat sitting at a table with a clean cloth and china cups, plates and real cutlery. All these things we had dreamed about. We had talked about food for many months but now our saliva flowed freely in anticipation as Bill named all the restaurants he knew in Calcutta. Our bodies were black from the sun; we carried scores of minor wounds and jungle sores and had been toughened by the rough living conditions. But we all shared a secret. We all carried the malaria bug and would succumb to an attack as soon as we ceased to take mepacrine tablets and the chances were, this would extend our leave. We would try to avoid joining the unit for as long as possible and not one of us would ever volunteer.

The rumor was that the length of overseas service had been reduced to six years and some said it would soon be five years, so we still had a long time to serve and nothing was certain. It was more than two years since we had drawn any pay and we were determined this leave would compensate for all the discomfort suffered. So, as soon as we received an advance of pay, travel vouchers and leave pass, Tom, Bill and I left camp shouldering our kit bags and clutching a packet of sandwiches provided for the journey. We were impatient and didn't wait for the transport provided into Kohima and thumbed a lift. It was a little over 100 miles and the journey took a day as the road was choked with military traffic.

That night we found a staging camp and slept on the floor of a basha with dozens of other leave men and, early next morning found a cooperative Indian driver who gave us a lift into Dimapur, a further journey of 70 miles, arriving at Tiffin, the same camp we had previously stayed in, on the journey into Burma. The same ginger haired sergeant greeted us and gave us a room.

Sheltered in the hills by huge Cedar trees we decided this would be as good a place as any to rest for a few days, but we didn't know then that the next move would take so long. After a week's rest with plenty to eat and drink, we decided we had had enough and moved on. So, we made enquiries at the transport office next door to the railway station for reservations for the rail journey. It was a pleasant half an hour walk from the camp to the railway siding and we expected to get seats almost immediately but when we arrived there, we were confronted by hundreds of men all with the same idea. Some of our own men had been told to wait and report every day and to take a chance that there was a spare seat. Or they would have to wait several weeks for a booking. When eventually we were able to get to the booking office we were told it would be at least three weeks before we could be guaranteed seats. They asked us to call again in three weeks time. We were comfortable in the transit camp and were not all that anxious to commence our leave, and no one bothered us.

"Jesus!" said Bill. "They bloody get us here but don't bloody care what happens to us, so sod the lot of them, let's stay at the camp until the bloody war's over."

However, another week at the transit camp and Tom and I had had enough. Bill hadn't been sober since we arrived at the camp, so we wondered if we should look for an alternate camp.

"What do you think of the idea of getting a lift by air?" asked Tom.

"We could go back to that airstrip at Palel and sort out those New Zealanders and see if they could suggest something, what do you think Bill? You never know, there may be a flight into Calcutta direct then they can stuff their fucking trains." This time we borrowed a jeep. We had no idea whose jeep it was. It was parked near the railway siding. It had no markings so we took it back to camp, loaded our kit and joined a convoy from Imphal and Palel. No one stopped us or asked any questions. Near the airstrip at Palel we hid the jeep and walked to the hangars, hoping to see someone we knew.

When we found them, the New Zealanders provided us with meals and beds and were generous with their liquor. But the chances of a flight into Calcutta were nil. It was the same in Imphal where the R.A.F. wanted everything in triplicate. On the other hand the Yanks would have taken us anywhere their planes went, including over the Hump into China. They suggested they take us to Comilla, where Army Headquarters was situated but we thought that might cause complications so we abandoned the idea, but, after a few days in Palel, we made our way back again to Dimapur and the ginger sergeant. We got accustomed to the early morning walk from the camp to the railway siding. It was another three weeks before we got seats on the train.

It was an uncomfortable journey, six hundred miles on hard seats and the temperature in the hundreds. The little single line meter gauge railway passes through thick jungle for seventy miles. The carriages were then man handled to cross the Brahmaputra by barge. Then to Guwahati and on to Dhubri, where we changed to the wide gauge system for Calcutta. The journey seemed endless and we hoped we would be able to avoid this part of the world in the future. Bill was even more determined to be our host.

"When we get to Cal." He said. "You chaps are coming with me to stay in my bungalow for a few days. I'll let them know, as soon as we get to the station and we'll have a few days rest to get over the journey." This, we readily agreed.

The taxi took us several miles out from the railway station to a European residential district on the Hooghly River. Bill's employers, where he was manager and chief engineer, had allowed him to retain his bungalow and servants and we had the best of everything. As Bill renewed old acquaintances, there was a constant stream of callers. They were all addicted to Scotch whiskey, which was in unlimited supply. Personally, I was never fond of whiskey, neither was Tom, but we went through the motions and enjoyed the company.

In a few days Bill insisted we should see something of Calcutta but wouldn't let us go half cocked. So, he arranged for a darzi (a local tailor) and a mochi (a local shoemaker) to measure us for suits and shoes. We had lightweight civvies for daytime wear and tuxedos for evening, as well as matching shirts, shoes and hats, all made to measure and, we understood, charged to his firm. To visit Chowringhee was a thrill for Tom and I. We joined several clubs under Bill's jurisdiction. We tried everything, saunas and clubs where we had massages, manicures and facial treatments. We were waited on by Chinese girls with iced fruit drinks and spent all our days just lounging about. By evening, we were ready for a seven-course meal in Firpos or some other restaurant and it became difficult to imagine there was a war on.

To limit the conflict of interests between British and American servicemen, Calcutta was divided into areas. A choice section of the Chowringhee district was out of bounds to British troops and had been made into an American saluting area. Large signs were in evidence announcing the commencement of this area that stated:

"All American troops will salute their officers and vice-versa whilst in the saluting area."

Other signs denoted certain areas to be out of bounds to British troops, but we were in civvies and could go anywhere. I suppose I was fortunate to have been able to visit clubs and places in the out-of-bounds areas and to be entertained by the Yanks and Bill's friends, who always insisted in picking up the bill. The air-conditioned Lighthouse cinema was a favorite rendezvous. Bill, with the eagerness of a schoolboy, hurried us from place to place and, after four weeks of alcoholic debauchery, I developed a permanent headache and started to run a temperature. The stench of rotting filth and dead bodies in the streets reminded me of the slaughter in Burma. I watched dead coolies floating past Bill's bungalow near the Hooghly River.

Our taxi collided with a dead cow in the road one day and everywhere we went, hundreds of coolies clutched at our clothes begging baksheesh. In Calcutta, hundreds of thousands of coolies live on the streets, are born and die there with no hope of ever doing anything else.

Back in the bungalow, it annoyed me that Bill spent most of the time in a drunken stupor. I longed to be on my own. One thing worried me and that was we would not get any mail until we officially reported to the leave centre. So, one day I said to Tom.

"You know Tom, any more of this and I'll be ill. I'd like to call it a day and report to the Leave Centre. What do you think?"

"I feel the same way Q. But we just can't walk out, after all the trouble Bill went to. I suggest we sound out Bill when he wakes up."

Bill's reaction was predictable. "Jesus Christ, we've only just fucking got here, those bastards won't miss us for a few weeks yet."

Then there was another party, and another, until one day, in desperation, Tom and I collected our kit and took a taxi to the Leave Centre. Bill was unconscious when we left. His bearer tried to rouse him but couldn't. He kept repeating: "Gone sahib! Finished."

We left him a note and we forgot to take note of his address. We never went back and never saw him again.

Beds were allocated to us in a spacious room on the first floor of the Museum building. The museum had been converted into a Rest Center for senior N.C.O.s and the facilities were immaculate. The temperature never dropped below ninety degrees Fahrenheit, but the huge fans, high up near the ceiling sent down a welcome breeze, in contrast to Bill's place that had air conditioning. A bearer was allocated to us and was on hand to supply all our needs. Because we perspired continuously and spent most of the time on our beds, fresh linen was necessary. We enjoyed a very early morning stroll in the park they called the Maiden, visited the Botanical Gardens and the Racecourse and took food down to the monkeys, who were running free everywhere. There were thousands on them.

We were always back for breakfast. It was near Christmas 1944, the second front was at a stalemate and the Japs were being chased out of Burma but it seemed the war would go on forever.

When Tom and I entered the Leave Centre after our early morning walk one day, we saw a notice about a recorded message to be broadcast by the B.B.C. in London. We immediately went along to the office and entered our names. They only wanted twenty sergeants and the list was soon filled. We were fortunate to be at the right place at the right time. We showered at least four times a day, and spent most of the day on our beds, covered only by a towel, dressing for meals and, if we weren't going anywhere, stripping off again. It was the only way to keep cool. The day we made the recording, transport was provided to take our party to the studios of Radio India. Here we prepared to record our messages. In the first place, each message had to be limited to twenty words, had to be in writing and approved. We spent most of that day and many sheets of paper preparing our messages, never getting it perfect. The first trial run was hilarious.

We lined up facing a B.B.C. announcer. He introduced us, giving our rank and name and quoting the names of the people we were calling. Then, taking our turn, we followed each other and read out our own message. Of course, our messages sounded ridiculous. We then made alterations and there was another trial run, then another, until we got it right. The first couple of hours were side splitting as we ridiculed each other's efforts.

You wouldn't believe it, but one man wanted to include a message for his pet dog with all the appropriate noises.

Once we were all word perfect, the process was speeded up to squeeze all the messages and the announcers' comments into the limited broadcast time allotted. It was very impersonal and we were fortunate to have been able to send a message home by this means. We completed prepaid postcards to tell our folks of the broadcast, the date and time being added in London when the cards were posted. I found out, when I at last reached home, that my wife and four year old son laughed and cried their way through the program, but my two year old daughter, not really appreciating the significance of the occasion, kept up a one sided conversation with a photograph of Daddy that she'd been given to keep her quiet.

During our stay at the Leave Centre, we only went abroad before breakfast or after dark. Calcutta, with its reeking millions, was a filthy city, full of beggary and bickering. There was a large variety of Hindu Gods enshrined in every conceivable place, blood red beetle nut stains covered the side walks and the half starved coolies were asleep everywhere. We found the Chinese Quarter to be the cleanest and abundant in the variety of merchandise. Any shopping expedition was time consuming, even in the largest stores as nothing was priced and one was expected to bargain and make a social occasion of it. The slightest suspicion of any interest was fatal, as the shopkeepers would follow us, with their goods until we were lost in the crowds. We saw both sides of life in Calcutta, after a month with Bill in the now out-of-bound areas, so we had no reason to wander far.

Two days before our four weeks leave was due to expire, I developed a high temperature. The next day, that is the last day of my leave, I was very sick and Tom had to send for the M.O. I was hoping Tom would also be sick because we had both ceased taking mepacrine tablets and hoped to develop malaria or sprue, as the local condition was called. The withdrawal symptoms, after two years of mepacrine produced a form of malaria rather like a common cold but with a high temperature and headache. Torn was disappointed, his temperature remained normal. The M.O., a Sikh, stinking of garlic, examined me and decided I should be hospitalized and ordered an ambulance. Tom now decided he would make a determined effort to get back to the old battery, so we said our goodbyes and he didn't follow me to the hospital. In a couple of days I was well and walking the wards. The large red 'Fourteen' overprinted on the medical records meant I had to have a number of tests. A week later the M.O. sent for me and said:

"I'm sorry quartermaster, I cannot send you back to your unit in your condition, so we have decided to get you to a convalescent hospital for a few days to see how you progress."

I was stunned as I had been feeling fit. The news gave me a sinking feeling.

"What's wrong sir?" I asked.

"You are underweight and have acute anemia and there may be something wrong with your liver. Tell me, have you been drinking a lot lately?"

"Not all that much sir, perhaps a little more than usual, but surely that wouldn't be anything serious?"

"No. I'm sure you'll be all right after a few days rest and treatment. I'm sorry, but I dare not send any of you Fourteenth army chaps back to duty unless you are one hundred per cent fit. So, I'm going to send you up to Darjeeling. You'll receive instructions in a few days, meantime you will stay in the hospital for rest and treatment."

So that was that. As it transpired, I would never rejoin my old regiment.

TWENTY

I WAS NOT AWARE of it at the time, but I was about to start my long journey home. It would take several months. The wheels of officialdom grind slowly. I had V.I.P. treatment for the journey to Darjeeling. By ambulance to the station, then aboard a first class air-conditioned sleeper reserved for the Red Cross. Two days later we changed to the tiny mountain railway with it's convex glass roof coaches. Stepping down into the coach I was swallowed in a soft upholstered lounge chair to view the ever-changing panorama. At the halt, half way up the mountain I began to acclimatize and, at four thousand feet above sea level we had refreshments. The few carriages were pushed by engines at both ends and, when climbing steeply, the sound of the safety ratchets going clickerty clapp, gave us assurance that we would not suddenly reverse downhill.

The view was breathtaking. It seemed as if we were suspended in mid air with a precipitous drop first to one side then the other, as the train shunted backwards and forwards. The valleys seemed bottomless. Through the clouds, we arrived at Darjeeling railway station, seven thousand feet above sea level. The air was rarefied and crisp and I found it harder to breath.

A tiny woman who could have been a grandmother, collected my kit, placed a cloth band around her forehead, squatted on the ground, leaned over backwards, took the weight and proceeded us up the steep hill and onto the road to our transport. I was already exhausted. The little old lady accepted a gift from me but there was no baksheesh up here. You won't believe it but I saw an upright piano moving slowly up the hill and, under it was another old woman. These sturdy mountain people had lost large numbers of their men in the war.

Like birds nests, the hospital buildings were perched on the side of the mountain slopes. From the window of the room allocated to me, I had a breathtaking view, even when sitting on my bed. I could see, about forty miles distant, the third highest mountain in the world, Kanchenjunga. It looked like an endless white wall that went up to the sky and changed color when not hidden by cloud.

The distant horizon was filled with snow-covered mountains. I couldn't see the other hospital buildings, but the wall of rock below my window dropped for four thousand feet into the valley. A stone staircase lead down to some departments of the hospital and the service rooms and dining rooms were on the same level. It was not a large hospital and all the troops I met were recovering from minor wounds or illness. I was put on a special diet to improve my blood count and got stronger every day. I learned to play badminton and became reasonably good at it, so much so, that I qualified for the hospital weekly championships. When horses were available, I went pony riding.

There were many interesting things to see up here on top of the world, with the museum and several well laid out parks, but the magnificent views from the hospital windows and grounds and the organized recreational activities tended to confine me to the hospital and, after an initial outburst of enthusiasm, I soon had no desire to wander abroad.

Early one morning with transport arranged by the hospital, a small party of us was taken to the top of Tiger Hill, to see the dawn over the Himalayas. We could see Mount Everest, even though it was over a hundred miles away.

It was a fantastic spectacle as the light patterns changed at sunrise. In the stillness of the crisp morning air, we watched the rainbows of color unfold across the sky. The first fan was a delicate mauve, and then oranges, reds and pinks, until the sun appeared and created clouds that obliterated the view. We had witnessed a miracle at dawn. This was such a contrast to a thousand miles away where men were hurtling explosives at each other in the mistaken belief that they were on the winning side.

On the first and third Tuesday of each month the house surgeon examined the inmates and it was routine for about a third to be ordered back to duty. After a month, the M.O. examined me and decided I was fit enough to go back to my unit. To confirm his findings, he decided to have another look at my eyes. As he walked away, he patted me on the head ostensibly to console me; fortunately the palm of his hand came in contact with a cyst growing in the middle of my scalp. The cyst was about an inch high and couldn't be seen through my hair.

"Hello, what's this?" he asked and examined it more closely. "We'll have to get rid of that before you go back to duty, has it given you any trouble?"

"Yes sir." I said. "It gets in the way when I wear my tin hat." Which was true.

"I'll give you a note to the surgeon. The surgery is just down the hill. Let's see now, I'll see you again in another two weeks. Meantime make your own arrangements to see the surgeon."

A badminton tournament prevented me from making an appointment with the surgeon for several days, but, when I did go down to the surgery, I was surprised to be confronted by a female, a full colonel, who assisted by a nurse, took the cyst out. Then the nurse bandaged me up. She placed gauze and a huge piece of cotton wool on top of my head and then proceeded to use dozens of yards of bandage, until, not only was my head covered, but also my eyes and ears. At the time I thought this was hilarious. The bandage could be lifted and put on again like a hat and this had advantages. I removed it indoors but always wore it outside except when playing badminton. At the next medical inspection I informed the M.O. the stitches would be removed before the end of the week and I was granted a further two weeks reprieve. This was useful as I was now an old established inmate and was able to take advantage of a number of trips to places of interest. Inevitably, it was back to duty at the next medical inspection and I received travel documents to proceed to a transit camp near Comilla. I wondered if I would ever get back to my old unit again. I had enjoyed the two months respite at Darjeeling and it was now five months since I went on leave from Imphal.

On arrival at the Comilla transit camp, a month old bulletin announced that any man who had completed four years or more continuous service overseas would now be repatriated to the U.K. but I still had about five months to wait, so I expected to be sent back to my unit at any time. I soon became convinced my old Regiment had replaced me as time passed and I had no news of a posting. Then another notice gave orders that the maximum time of service overseas was reduced to three years and eight months. I wrote home with the good news. It was April 1945. In this huge camp, hundreds of men were arriving and departing every day and the queue to read the notices was never ending. It was another three weeks before my name appeared on orders to proceed to Poona, which is only a short distance from Bombay.

I purchased two white naval kit bags, as they were twice the size of the army issue, had my number, rank, and name stenciled on them and proceeded to comb the bazaars for gifts to take home. Within a few days of arrival at Poona, all those men still alive who had traveled out in August 1941 were gathered together and early one morning we entrained for Bombay. Within hours we were on aboard S.S. Strathmore. It was very crowded but I was happy to be on our way home at last.

I was lucky to be on D deck and I didn't mind the lack of space. It was estimated there were six thousand troops on board, six times the number the ship was designed for. There were only eighty-seven of us gunners left from the original draft of nearly five hundred and we were thankful to have survived. It was hot and humid when we reached the top of the gangway where we were each given an envelope, unsealed, from Army Headquarters.

The letter, on cheap newsprint, was as follows:

22nd Jan 1945.

Tac H.Q.

Allied Land Forces, South East Asia.

A

PERSONAL MESSAGE

FROM

THE COMMANDER-IN-CHIEF

Before you leave for home, I would like to thank you for the good work you have done out here.

I well realize what it must have meant to you, and to your family at home, to be kept here, while others were able to leave as soon as their time was up.

I wish you a good leave and the best of luck in the future You can be proud to have played your part in this hard campaign for the reconquest of Burma,

(signed)

Oliver Leese

Lieutenant General

Most men destroyed their copies of the letter in disgust as they perspired under the burden of their kit. I still have my copy.

No sooner had the boat sailed than queues began to form for extra cups of tea, cigarettes and various merchandise, suitable for gifts. Everything was ridiculously cheap and tax free, and where things were rationed we joined the tail of the queue again. There wasn't much else to do. Tom and I joined members of the crew on A deck which was officially out of bounds to all troops but like the crew, we wore only gym shorts, we played cards and slept up there at night. The crew helped us collect many things to take home and saved us the time in lining up.

We were on A deck one day playing cards and with us was a warrant officer I had dealings with in Quetta. I forget his name but knew him as Ginger. That day he told us a sorry story about his private life. His wife had left him and had two children by another man since he came overseas. His parents had been killed in an air raid and he confessed he now had V. D. He didn't want to go home, as he had no home to go to now. Then he stood up, climbed the rail by the lifeboat and jumped. We didn't hear any splash and it was a minute before the alarm was sounded and although the ship circled for an hour, we never found him and we continued the journey.

We celebrated V. E. day in the middle of the Red Sea. At last the war in Europe was over. The heat on deck now was almost unbearable.

The victory was celebrated by an issue of a bottle of beer, most of which shot up to the cabin ceilings.

After a short pause at Tufic, we went through the Suez canal where sand dunes on each side of the boat seemed near enough to touch. It was a miracle the boat didn't go aground as it sucked up the water and appeared to travel on the sandy bottom, followed by a wall of water which seemed to be all that was propelling it along.

Camels walked along the sand dunes bordering the canal. The life style of the natives hadn't changed for thousands of years. The ninety miles of canal passed all too quickly as we crowded the decks. A brief call at Suez and we were in the Mediterranean. It was cooler on deck now and we were able to sunbathe. Soon we saw the sand colored buildings of Malta and as we steamed westwards, were told by the crew that the Windsor Castle, the ship we had traveled out on, was struck by an aerial torpedo about a hundred miles north west of Algiers on 23rd March 1943 and sank. There were 2699 troops and 289 crew on board but only one life was lost.

We dropped anchor under the shadow of the rock of Gibraltar and watched the monkeys watching us. Then we were in the Bay of Biscay and it was raining. It rained all the way to Liverpool. A thin cold mist was falling as the boat dropped anchor in the Mersey and for the first time in years, we were pleased to wear our greatcoats.

Customs men came aboard almost immediately. They ransacked the cabins and we heard that officers were being asked to pay large sums in duty. All other ranks were paraded past customs officers and each, in turn, was asked if they had anything to declare. It soon became obvious this was only routine, as they wanted to get rid of us as quickly as possible. When my turn came, I told the truth that I had three thousand cigarettes and the customs man told me to piss off. Whilst our kit bags were being lowered onto a barge we had a quick medical, then rushed to join our kit down the ladders. The boat was riding at anchor in midstream and, as the distance lengthened and the barge pulled away, we were happy. Soon we were on the train.

We were allowed to send home a prepaid telegram and I hoped to arrive before it.

Next morning, at Woolwich, we had to cart all our kit to the Royal Artillery barracks. I hired a coster barrow; my kit bags were so heavy.

All we did here was collect leave documents, pay and ration books and then it was a rush to London Bridge Station, taxi to Fenchurch Street and another train to Benfleet. No one offered to help me with my kit as I dragged it about and I was the only passenger to alight at Benfleet. To get transport here was like raising the dead.

Tired, unshaven and annoyed by all the delays, my heart was filled with joy when I had sight of the bungalow that was to be my home.

A "Welcome Home" sign was nailed over the front entrance and the noise of the taxi alerted my family who had been waiting for many hours.

Full of embarrassment at the sight of each other, my family devoured me and I them. I embraced my wife and son I had not seen for four years and my new daughter.

EPILOGUE

WHO PISSED IN the officer's rum?

I was walking down our main street one morning in early 1972 when I heard a voice call "Hi Q!"

On the opposite side of the road was a man I recognized. He waved and shouted, "Who pissed in the officer's rum, Q?" I crossed and shook his outstretched hand. On the pavement, we talked about India and Burma and the men who perished, of the filth, disease and wretchedness of all those hopeless months cut off in Central Burma surrounded by Japanese troops. I remembered this chap as a gunner on number one gun. He knew me, but frankly I wouldn't have recognized him in other circumstances. When I left him he told me where he worked and I promised to look him up, but when I did, some weeks later, the business had changed hands, and I hate to admit it, I had forgotten his name and never saw him again.

Normally we have the right to choose our way of life, if we make sacrifices it is our own choice. Life is no more than an argument with death anyway and there is reasonable hope to postpone the decision, but in war we have no control. We are ordered and with the fear of being labeled a coward, we click our heels and eyes closed, we rush headlong towards eternity.

No mere words can describe the bestiality, deprivation, degradation and suffering of the men of the "Forgotten Army" in Burma.

I have endeavored to record incidents as they happened and apologize for the many omissions.

George Spill

MY LAST NIGHT WITH GEORGE

THE LAST NIGHT I spent with my father, he told me three family secrets. He was 97 and before his next birthday, when I planned to see him again in New Zealand, he would be dead. We had finished our meal we had cooked together; lamb chops, potatoes and silver beet followed by canned peaches and ice cream.

He sat in his favorite chair and started talking, his eyes half closed.

"I killed 46 Japs one night." He had never mentioned numbers before. I had heard him tell stories how he had woken up the next morning in a foxhole in Burma with bodies sprawled over barbed wire and in the trenches next to him, his crate of grenades empty, his gun still smoking hot. Then he continued. I did not want to interrupt him because I had never heard him speak like this, ever.

"We were Jewish once. Did you know?" He had never even hinted at this before. "My father gathered the family together after the Sunday meal and said we were too poor to be Jews and we weren't going to be Jews anymore."

"Oh." Was all I could say. I wanted to add that I was born into the poorest Jewish family in England and it's been kept a secret all my life! What was going on?

"I could have been told this earlier, Dad. Not when I'm in my 50's. Remember how I was on a spiritual quest when I was 18 and tried everything; Krishna, Buddha, Zen, Baha'i Faith? I knew something was missing. It would've helped."

He was gazing faraway and I was not sure he had heard or wanted to hear me.

"You were born two years before. But we had to abort you, otherwise mother would have died."

I had heard stories of my mother being in hospital with high blood pressure and what a difficult pregnancy she had. But I did not know I was the second attempt.

The plan was to have another baby in 1948. My father came back from Burma in 1945 and this gave them enough time to save up and move into a bigger house. My parents wanted to have a child they could both watch grow up. My father missed out on his two older children's first years.

Reluctant Q is my father's story. He used to tell pieces of it after Sunday lunch when I was growing up. My mother used to make fun of him when he started: "When I was in Burma."

Like the time he found a young soldier who had just been hit with shrapnel from a Japanese artillery attack. The man was lying with his intestines falling out of his shirt. My father gave him a shot of morphine. He was crying in pain and passed out. My father realized there was no way they could save him in the jungle. So my father gave him another dose of morphine and held his hand as he slipped away.

George was a reluctant soldier. The worst times were nights in Burma when suicide squads of Japanese soldiers, intent on victory or a glorious Samurai death, infiltrated his artillery unit. My father manned a gun post that was part of an intricate crossfire pattern defending their few surviving field artillery guns. He had a crate of grenades, sometimes two, a bottle of rum and plenty of ammunition. He would wake up the next morning to discover bodies strewn across the no man's land. Sometimes other guns were blown up and trenches overrun.

An unlikely war hero, my father, as quartermaster to his battery, made sure his men were well equipped. They had all the rum they could drink. He might have worn rags, had long hair and a beard in the hills of Burma during the worst of the fighting, but he had enough ammo, some water and American K rations. Enough to tide them over till their next airdrop with no parachutes. Parachutes were needed on the Western front. This was the Forgotten Army.

My father could not save the lives of his friends. Everyone he was close to died. Most of his commanding officers died. Most of his fellow soldiers died. His best friend Nick (named Johnny in the book) was blown up by a direct hit from a Japanese artillery shell.

I would be named after my father's best friend.

George was highly motivated to get back to his wife he had just married, a son he had only seen a few times and a daughter who was a stranger to him.

Despite the odds, George managed to walk out of the jungle and eventually board a troop ship sailing back to England.

This is his story.

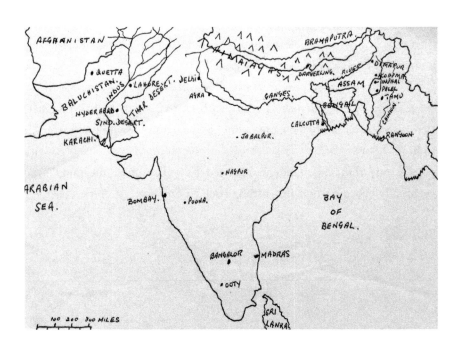

George's map of India and Burma. He was an excellent draughtsman and when he retired he took up painting.

George with three stripes, the photo was taken
somewhere near the Afghanistan border.

George and Nick somewhere near Afghanistan.
Nick was his closest friend and was killed by a direct
artillery attack. I would be named after him.

The box of medals that arrived after the War. George was bitter
about the wasted years he had endured for King and country. He was
unable to complete his accountancy exams when he returned. He
had two small children to feed and was economically disadvantaged
from the low Army pay he had received. He put the medals away
and did not look at them for a long time. He felt all the sacrifice and
bloodshed went unrecognized by the British government not just for
himself but for all his dead mates he had left behind in the jungle.

The Burma Star. If you were in Burma, you got one.

The four medals George received in the mail. George tells the story how as the highest surviving N.C.O., he was assigned to award medals to his unit in Burma. He could have given himself the Military medal; instead he recommended a number of medals to the severely wounded in his battery.

George salutes at the War Museum in Auckland, New Zealand. I had
walked him around the museum and given him a pep talk about how
important his role was during the War and what a hero I thought he
was. When I asked for his photo he spontaneously saluted. I think
he was serious although he did have his Benny Hill moments.

George eating our last meal we cooked together,
lamb chops and veges, before he dropped the three
family bombshells as revealed in the book.

George Spill walks off into the sunset in Orewa, New Zealand.

Born a cockney in London, George Spill fell in love with New Zealand after he met a couple of Kiwis who crashed in the Burmese jungle. After saving enough money to pay for his family's passage and buy a new house, he sailed with his family to New Zealand. He built several thriving businesses and lived happily with his wife Olive and three children. Despite losing his wife to Alzheimer's, he was able to live a productive life till he was 97 years old. He loved to take long walks, painted in oils and was an expert bridge player. His younger son Nick promised to publish George's war memoir, Reluctant Q.

ABOUT NICK SPILL

NICK SPILL LIVES in South Florida where he works as a criminal defense investigator and specializes in major crimes. He encouraged his father to write his Burma war memoirs and they talked extensively about the book before his father's death. He has added to the narrative and believes this is an accurate chronicle of the tragedy and comedy that his father lived through. Other books by Nick Spill include The Way of the Bodyguard, a non-fiction account of protecting the famous, the infamous and the anonymous.

OTHER BOOKS BY NICK SPILL
AVAILABLE ON AMAZON

The Way of the Bodyguard
(e-book and print editions)

Cactus Pricks and Dolphin Kicks

The Palace in TriBeca

Printed in Great Britain
by Amazon

30197401R00109